I0832299

THE HIGHER LAW,

IN ITS

RELATIONS TO CIVIL GOVERNMENT:

WITH PARTICULAR REFERENCE TO

SLAVERY,

AND

THE FUGITIVE SLAVE LAW.

BY WILLIAM HOSMER.

"THE LORD IS OUR JUDGE, THE LORD IS OUR LAW-GIVER, THE LORD IS OUR KING."—*Isaiah.*

AUBURN:
DERBY & MILLER.
1852.

E

TO

WILLIAM H. SEWARD,

LATE GOVERNOR OF THE STATE OF NEW-YORK, AND NOW SENATOR OF THE UNITED STATES:

SIR—The permission which I have, to inscribe this volume to you, is gratefully acknowledged. The title was suggested by incidents connected with yourself, and it was therefore fit that the work should go out to the world with the alliance of your name. But other reasons were not wanting: the eminent ability and patriotism with which, on all occasions, whether in the executive chair, or in the national legislature, or at the bar, you have defended the rights of humanity, entitle you to the lasting gratitude of your countrymen, and render it proper for them, in every suitable way, to express their high regard for your services.

THE AUTHOR.

PREFACE.

It affords me no small pleasure to speak for those who cannot speak for themselves. The slave, manacled and dumb, is forbidden to assert, either by word or deed, his right to the inalienable and priceless inheritance of liberty. In this sad condition, who shall more deeply sympathize with the bondman, or more strenuously advocate his claims, than the ministers of Him who came "to proclaim liberty to the captives, and the opening of the prison doors to them that are bound?" But there is more than a work of mercy involved in this issue. The highest principles of the Christian faith have been impugned, and if ministers were inclined to stand aside, they could not, without an utter forfeiture of character. It is their business to proclaim the Higher Law, and the Higher Law as paramount to all other laws. They are heralds of the kingdom of God, and when that kingdom is contemned, they must appear in its defence, or Christ is betrayed in the house of his friends. This task is incidental to the statesman, but not to the minister, for he is charged with this very work—he is set for the defence of the Gospel.

The reader will find here a full and consecutive development of those principles which, in another relation to the public, I have felt, and still feel, it my duty to maintain. Others may view the subject differently, but I cannot have a clear conscience and remain silent in the presence of such injustice to man, and such impiety to God. "First pure, then peaceable," should be our motto. The question is no longer diminutive and local. It fills the whole land, and compels every man to take a position on one side or the other—against slavery or against liberty. There is no longer any neutral ground.

More commonly the occurrences by which great principles are tested, are in themselves of slight importance. But in the present instance the reverse is strikingly true. The very existence of the church and of the government, is involved in the now pending question of emancipation. To all human appearance, we must either put away oppression, or yield the high religious and political advantages we now hold.

AUBURN, July 5, 1852.

CONTENTS.

CHAPTER XVII.

CHAPTER XVIII.

THE HIGHER LAW.

THE HIGHER LAW.

CHAPTER I.

INTRODUCTION.

If human laws are the highest, they certainly ought to be obeyed at any and every hazard. Their agreement or disagreement with the law of God is a matter of no consequence: they may be right, or they may be wrong, but in either case, if we acknowledge their supremacy, the subject must obey, and as much in one case as in the other. This conclusion cannot be resisted, if the premises on which it rests are allowed to stand. Our present inquiry, therefore, is one fraught with the deepest interest to human welfare. It lies at the very foundation of duty. The question is alike important to civil and to religious obligations.

It is obvious that no *ex cathedra* decision on this subject can avail any thing; the question of supremacy—if supremacy exists anywhere—must be determined by an appeal to facts. Mere hypothesis will not answer in so serious a matter: neither will prescription, nor tradition. We can rest on nothing short of those substantial elements of knowledge of which our own consciousness takes cognizance.

Some may consider the question already settled—a foregone conclusion—and object to re-opening it. We once considered it so, at least so far as this country is concerned; but recent circumstances have materially changed this opinion. The supremacy of the Divine law is no longer an unquestioned truth among us. Of this we need no other proof than the fact, that when a distinguished citizen of this state lately declared, in the Senate of the United States, that "there is a higher law than the constitution,"* the declaration, instead of eliciting an instant and cordial approval, drew down upon him a storm of invective. For the utterance of a truth which must ever be fundamental to Christianity, he was charged with seditious and treasonable designs against the government of the country. These charges were not hastily made, in the excitement of debate, but were the cool, deliberate sentiments of men who

* "It is true, indeed, that the national domain is ours. It is true it was acquired with the valor and with the wealth of the whole nation. But we hold, nevertheless, no arbitrary power over it. We hold no arbitrary authority over any thing, whether acquired lawfully, or seized by usurpation. The constitution regulates our stewardship; the constitution devotes the domain to union, to justice, to defence, to welfare, and to liberty. But there is a higher law than the constitution, which regulates our authority over the domain, and devotes it to the same noble purposes. The territory is a part, no inconsiderable part, of the common heritage of mankind, bestowed upon them by the Creator of the universe. We are his stewards, and must so discharge our trust as to secure in the highest attainable degree their happiness."—*Speech of* GOV. SEWARD *in the Senate, March* 12, 1850.

speak only what they think. They were made again and again, in Congress and out of Congress, by secular men and ecclesiastics, from the press and the pulpit. As a specimen of them we give the following from the *Washington Republic*—a leading political paper, published in the District of Columbia:

"We have endeavored to show into what labyrinths of error a statesman runs when he acknowledges a higher law than the constitution, and his oath to support it. We need not dwell more on that point. We have seen that Mr. Seward has culled the field of fanatical declamation of its choicest flowers; and in admirable English and neatly elaborated periods, avowed an independence of constitutional obligation, which, if followed by others, must end in the annihilation of all government, all law, all rights. Every other man in the United States has just as much right to set up a law in his breast, 'higher than the constitution,' as Mr. Seward has. And as constitutional law is the highest man can make, it follows that every man may break municipal and legislative law with yet greater impunity. Anarchy and bloodshed; the law of the strong arm; the law of the sword; the Lynch law, and kindred enormities, are the sequence of a doctrine like this. Anarchy, in its worst form; and the law of force, in its cruelest aspect."

When such language as this is allowed to pass unrebuked, it is time for those who believe in a Higher Law to state their views without equivocation or evasion, and with whatever of argument they can command. Unless we greatly mistake, the first principles of both natural and revealed religion are openly assailed. It is barely possible, however, that those who hold the sentiments contained in the above extract, only intend to assert that human enactments have a conditional supremacy. They mean, perhaps, no more than this—that in the arrangement of Providence, the laws of man are assigned as an ultimate standard of right, to which it is the will of God that all men should bow as to himself. But this explanation, though it may relieve the case of that stark infidelity which must otherwise attach to it, is by no means satisfactory. It is scarcely less objectionable in any respect, and probably more mischievous in practice, than avowed skepticism. I shall not here enter upon the argument by which this phase of the question is so easily met and refuted, as it will come up more properly in another place; but it may be well to state, in the outset, that all conclusions based upon such an explanation are utterly sophistical. No higher law, existing under such modifications, can have any effect upon the conduct of men. We may as well—and better—have infidelity without this poor disguise. The thin drapery of religion thrown over the disgusting form of atheism, may deceive the unsuspecting, but cannot change the nature of things, nor lessen the disastrous consequences of error.

These statements sufficiently disclose the motives which have led to this work. The writer has no wish to engage in a semi-political controversy; he is quite willing to leave politics to those to whom such things more immediately belong. But a full conviction that a blow is aimed—whether maliciously or ignorantly, he does not say—at the very existence of religion and the best interests of the state, leaves him not at liberty to decline the investigation. Nor is it probable that the discussion will soon end. The burden of determining anew, or at least of re-asserting what are the rights respectively of civil government and of Christianity, seems to be thrown upon this age. The lessons of history appear to exert little influence, and the great problem of human rights must be solved once more. May it be, not as heretofore, on fields of blood and carnage; but with the more powerful, yet bloodless, weapons of truth and righteousness.

In conducting this discussion we shall not be confined to any single aspect of the subject; much less to a survey of the Higher Law in the abstract. The existence and claims of such a law constitute an all-pervading truth. We shall find traces of them in every thing around us—in man, in civil government, in the external world, and in whatever presents itself to our observation. This is not simply a question of jurisprudence, or of ethics, or of theology; but rather of all combined—of truth in general.

CHAPTER II.

THE HIGHER LAW.

SECTION I.

MANIFESTATION OF THE HIGHER LAW.

The law of God is indicated in the following ways:

1. By the natural constitution of things.
2. By the course of Providence.
3. By direct revelation.

NATURE.

That man is not left wholly to self-regulation, is a truth so obvious as to require no proof. That he is a being affected by influences beyond his control, has never been denied, and never can be by any sane mind. It may be difficult to determine what these influences are, or to what extent they are to be regarded in the practice of life; but the fact of their existence admits of no dispute. One or two facts in relation to physical existence will illustrate this remark. Death, though it may be accidental, cannot by any possibility be prevented. As an ultimate event, it is absolutely certain. The mode of subsistence, however it may be varied, is, after all, essentially the same in all human beings, and wholly unalterable. Man can subsist only by nourishment, received into the system through the appropriate organs of nutrition. Again, he must have air to breathe, or death immediately ensues. The circulation of the blood is another condition of life, equally incontestible.

That the constitution of things clearly unfolds a higher law than man can ordain, has been partly shown in the preceding observations. But the argument may be extended much farther. No one will pretend that the several endowments and conditions of human nature do not point to certain correspondencies in practical life. For instance, the demand for food evidently points to some exertion to procure food, or, in other words, to the great law of industry so clearly revealed in the Scriptures—"In the sweat of thy face shalt thou eat bread, till thou return unto the ground." The social feelings as evidently indicate that man was made for society, and point to the marriage relation, no less distinctly than the written word, which says, "It is not good that the man should be alone." "Let every man have his own wife." Again, the desire of happiness prevalent in every human breast, connected as this desire is with a consciousness of dependence upon others, intimates the duty of reciprocal kindness, as plainly as the law, which says, "Thou shalt love thy neighbor as thyself." These are only a few of the numberless instances in which the will of the Creator is made unmistakably plain, by the constitution that he has given us, or the circumstances in which he has placed us. It would not be possible to misapprehend the design in either of the instances referred to: at all events, it would be quite as impossible to do so as it would to mistake the use of our natural faculties, and attempt to walk on the hands instead of the feet, or to hear with the eyes instead of the ears.

Now, the use of these simple truths is this: they show, beyond all controversy, that at least in some things we are bound by conditions—that is, laws—which we must abide, because it is not in our power to set them aside. That is to say, physical existence acknowledges a higher law, whether we intellectually and morally acknowledge it or not.

The question then, so far as relates to some kind of a law, is settled.

But we are in search of a moral law, and until this is found, it does not become positively certain that man may not do as he pleases in things of a moral character. If we admit the claims of Christianity, the argument is at an end, for that is professedly a revelation of the law of God. Or if we even admit the existence of God, the result is the same. The nature of God makes him the Supreme Lawgiver. He could not be God if he were not the highest; and if the highest in any thing, then is he the highest in every thing—in morals as well as in physics. But if even his existence is denied, the conclusion yet remains good, that there must be a higher law. We have seen that physical life, or nature, is "held fast in fate," and this, irrespective of all questions touching the existence or non-existence of a Supreme Being. Our moral nature, whatever it may be, is circumscribed by limits and conditions strictly analogous. As we cannot resist death, nor live without nourishment, so neither can we carry virtue, or any crime, beyond a given extent. Man's will is not supreme in the department of morals. He cannot love and hate the same being at the same time; nor can he be good and bad at the same time. He cannot blend vice and virtue, nor change the nature of the one or the other. What is right, is right in spite of him; and what is wrong, is wrong in spite of him. Hence it is clear that in these particulars he is controlled by a law above himself, the conditions of which he is unable to change, and the authority of which he is equally unable to throw off. He is, moreover, unable to separate himself from moral character; his nature has in it the elements of morality, and he may be either good or bad, but he cannot avoid both of these conditions, and remain exempt from either virtue or vice. Nor can the influence of numbers make any difference in his moral relations. The united voice of the race might decree that vice should be virtue, and virtue vice; or, that neither vice nor virtue should have any existence, and the decree would be just as powerless as if it had affirmed that man should not die.

PROVIDENCE.

Providence is the term which we employ to designate the course of nature. The constitution of things proclaims for what they are fitted, but it does not necessarily determine what their practical operation shall be. Not that the things themselves have power to change their destiny, but that the Author of nature may not be governed by what seems to us the natural use of the things he has made. Is the Divine providence, then, in accordance with the natural constitution of things, or not? The affirmative of this question is certain, beyond all contingency. We have already seen that the great laws of man's physical and moral being are sovereign—that they are not subject to his will, and cannot be set aside by him—that they are woven into his nature, and must have their course. The question now arises—Have these laws, thus wrought into the constitution of man, declined? Are there any exceptions?—and if so, do they indicate that the universal law is not steadily maintained in the government of the world? The course of Providence seems to be eminently in harmony with the creative law. Death is no more incidental than it was at first; mortality prevails over all men with the same undeviating certainty that it did over the first generation. The mode of subsistence is likewise unvaried. Food and air, and the operation of the vital functions, are just as indispensable now as they ever were. Remoter laws also are equally unimpaired. The earth still yields its harvest only to the hand of industry; the social relations still have their full attractive force, and confer the same benefits as of old. Nor is charity less indispensable than it used to be. In these respects all things remain as they were from the beginning; the creation and perpetuation of the race involve precisely the same principles.

The moral administration of Providence is marked by the same exact regard to constitutional principles. Man has not been able to surpass himself; his crimes and his virtues are still those of man. He has not done either good or bad as he might have done, had it been possible for him, at will, to rise above or sink below the powers which God has given him. Good is good, and bad is bad—now as heretofore. Virtue finds its reward, and vice its punishment, with as much certainty as at any former period—that is, invariably. We say, invariably, because there are only slight exceptions in the actual result, and none at all in the administrative law. Any apparent irregularity which we may detect, grows out of the almost incomprehensible sweep of retributive Providence. This is only a preliminary state, and the conduct of its affairs must, in some degree, be modified by considerations connected with a future world. But this is no abatement of order—no variation of principle—no change of law. The effect may be delayed, but the cause does not cease to operate. The culprit may be shielded for a time, yet vengeance is sure to overtake him, unless he repents. God does not relinquish his purpose. We conclude, then, that the course of Providence is affirmative of all natural indications. The Governor of the universe is carrying out the designs of the Creator.

REVELATION.

Of the will of God, as manifested in revelation, but little need be said. It is too plain and too decisive to require comment in a preliminary inquiry like this. If we admit revelation at all, we admit it in its character of law. That the revealed word of God sanctions and upholds all the great principles embodied in the constitution of the world, is a self-evident truth. The Bible is the Higher Law, in fact and in form. It is a formal announcement of the Divine will as the Divine will. In it God, in his character of Creator, and Upholder, and Governor of all things, prescribes to man the rules of duty, accompanied by all necessary prohibitions and penalties. What is silently expressed by creation and providence, in the Scriptures is made to assume the shape of speech. That more is comprehended in the written word than in the teachings of nature, was to be expected, and does not vary the case, since the difference is only in degree and not in kind. As in nature the law is expressed in the work, so in revelation the law is contained in the word. Hence the terms word and law are often used interchangably in the sacred writings. The creature could not exist without its inherent constitutional or organic law; neither can the word of God exist without its essential qualities—supremacy, holiness, wisdom. benevolence. This word is undoubtedly the brightest, latest, fullest manifestation of law that can be conceived. It is God breaking the silence of eternity with an audible utterance of his own character and purposes. Where nature but hinted, this gives a full exposition; and so copious is the information, that nothing but irreverent curiosity or selfish pride can ask for more. It is true that Divinity assumed the office of Lawgiver, when the unalterable relations of things were fixed; that, however, was not all the law man required—nature's code was not enough to meet all his wants—he had hopes and fears that could not be satisfied till life and immortality, with all their conditions, were brought to light through the gospel. He needed not a higher law than had been stamped upon nature, but a reaffirmation of the original decree, with the addition of such provisions and illustrations as are rendered necessary by the present lapsed condition of humanity. Having this, he needs no more.

SECTION II.

CHARACTER OF THE HIGHER LAW.

In characterizing the Divine law, we shall of course have reference to its most perfect form—to the written word—and especially to that written upon tables of stone. But where shall we begin! The law itself is a wonder—an aggregate of wonders. All Scripture was given by inspiration, but the law was written with the finger of God. From this assemblage of magnificent requirements it is not easy to select, even for the purpose of admiration—so fully has Godhead left its stamp on every part. All is equally excellent, and equally authoritative—not one jot or tittle shall fail. Resistance in the least, is resistance in the greatest; "for whosoever shall keep the whole law, and yet offend in one point, he is guilty of all." It is here as in the chain of nature—

"——— whatever link you strike,
Tenth or ten-thousandth, breaks the chain alike."

Each precept is clothed with all the authority of the Eternal, and disobedience, however slight, sets that authority at defiance.

It will readily be admitted that this law is an adumbration of its author. God himself shines forth in every word. The law of God—whether we understand thereby the several precepts he has given, or the Scriptures generally—is a revelation of his mind, and will, and nature, incomparably more perfect than could be obtained by any other means in this life. We must not, however, forget that this law is not himself. It may be like him—a transcript of his mind—but it is no more than a transcript. So man bears the image of God, but man is not God.

Thus, while we do not deify the law, we nevertheless make it the perfect work of a perfect God. We do not worship the law, but accept it as a bright and beneficent expression of the Divine character, and as the only sufficient rule for the government of conduct. The points to which we wish more particularly to direct attention are the following:

SUPREMACY.

Man's nature being subordinate, can never rise above the Divine law. A law of God once given, remains in force till repealed by Him who gave it. We cannot exempt ourselves, because the relation between Him and us cannot be changed. Between the creature and the Creator—the finite and the Infinite—there must ever be the same undiminished difference. In Him centres the right to rule, and in us the necessity to obey. He is ever God, and we are ever his creatures. There can be no change of natures. He cannot cease to be God, nor we to be men. This, duly considered, must forever establish his claims, not barely in the things where we have his special direction, but as our Supreme Governor, whose authority is always to be acknowledged, even though we may not be able to ascertain his will.

Men have ingeniously sought to evade the force of this law by alleging that its supremacy is confined to particular departments of duty. It has been affirmed, for instance, that in matters of faith or religion, the Bible is the highest authority, but not in matters of state. This is a miserable evasion. The Divine supremacy extends to every thing, and to one thing as fully as to another. Matters of religion are no more under God's direction or authority than matters of state. His supremacy is universal and unlimited, throughout all time and all space. But it is claimed that institutions existing by Divine authority are exponents of the Divine will, and that we are to receive their decrees as the decree of God. This, also, is a fallacy. Before God there are no institutions of the kind now alluded to; he has erected no infallibilities of a corporate or social character. He has not delegated his authority so as to sanction an infringement of his own immaculate government. All institutions, and all men, in their public as well as their private acts, are subject to the law of God. If institutions had discretionary authority—if they might do as they pleased, without reference to the Bible—then their enactments, though wrong, might be obligatory. But institutions of all kinds are as strictly bound as individuals, and they have not the slightest authority to do wrong themselves; much less have they authority to compel others to do wrong. The law of God in reference to all things human, is *semper et ubique eadem*—always and everywhere the same. How preposterous, then, to allege Divine authority for a wanton exercise of power! There is no power but of God. Men have his authority to do right, but they never can have his authority to do wrong, or to force others to do wrong. This wonderful law is over all equally. The king and the subject, the prince and the peasant, are alike amenable for their conduct to the one Lawgiver, who is able to save or to destroy. Most healthful would the entertainment of this essential truth be to the heaven-defying multitudes who arrogate to themselves entire self-control, because God has laid upon them certain duties involving the exercise of common-sense.

HOLINESS.

The purity of the law is another of its peculiarities. "The law is holy, and the commandment holy, and just, and good." It must be so, for a holy God could not be the author of an unholy law. His law must be, like himself, infinitely pure. Nor does this wonderful purity flow from any contingency; it is not an incident attaching to the Divine law. God made the law in accordance with the eternal and immutable integrity of his own nature. He could not make an unholy law. It is this essential attribute of his law which makes it so unwelcome to wicked men. To all such, the law is a voice of condemnation, because their deeds are evil. The pure requirements of the Most High impose a sovereign restraint upon corrupt nature. Hence, the rebellion among the wicked—they cannot endure commands that check so effectually the cherished propensities of their depraved hearts. "The carnal mind is enmity against God—it is not subject to the law of God, neither indeed can be." It is this amazing truth that gives such especial importance to the doctrine of regeneration. "Without holiness no man shall see the Lord," because no man, without this qualification, can be at peace with him. God and the wicked are necessarily and eternally enemies—except as the latter may be saved from their sins. The conditions of the Divine administration are reformation or destruction. The sinner must repent or perish.

WISDOM.

Here only has law an indisputably perfect adaptation. Its application to man is especially remarkable. Human laws bear heavily upon us at many points. Ignorance, and selfishness, and depravity, have corrupted legislation, till earth groans under legalized wickedness. Not so with the code of heaven. Its strictest prohibitions, its severest penalties, and its highest injunctions, are alike admirably adapted to the wants of humanity. Man needs just such restraints, just such penalties, and just such commands. Not one enactment too few, not one too many; not one too lax, not one too stringent. What a harmonious blending of authority with constitutional wants! Verily, none but the Creator could have instituted such control. The governing power is applied to man as gently as the seasons are to nature, or as the elements are to his body. The air we breathe, the light which we see, the water which laves us, the fire that warms us, and the food which nourishes us, are not more carefully and wisely adjusted to our physical powers, than are these written laws to the government of our moral nature. Let the skeptic reflect on this mysterious gentleness of Omnipotence, and learn to adore a power which never exerts itself amiss.

BENEVOLENCE.

The law is essentially good, and therefore benevolent. It is not impracticable, nor unreasonable. It is an infallible rule for the conduct of life. It is the exact truth in reference to duty—the true secret of success—the only key to happiness and heaven. Those who would enter into life must keep the commandments. These commandments are not arbitrary tests of authority, imposed by unlimited power; but the true theory of life, comprising directions for the certain attainment of the highest felicity. Such a rule is priceless, because it sets aside all error, and prevents the waste and misdirection of human energies.

SECTION III.

OBJECTS OF THE HIGHER LAW.

The general design of the law will readily be inferred from its character. A law so high and holy, so truthful and wise, could not have a low purpose, nor any purpose less exalted than the conservation of those to whom it was given. The law accomplishes this object by affording to all, protection, instruction and ennoblement.

1. Human laws may work oppression instead of protection; but the law of God neither oppresses any, nor allows any to be oppressed. It protects the rights of all, and this too in all respects. By banishing every sin, and demanding universal holiness, it ensures to each and all equal and exact justice. This law leaves nothing to human caprice — it knows neither high nor low, but places all on a level, and requires every one to do according to his ability. The strong cannot trample upon the weak, for all rights are equally sacred before God, "who, without respect of persons, judgeth according to every man's work." No institution, whether Divine or human, can depart from this protective and immaculate character, without corruption. Whatever oppresses or injures, is at war with God and his creatures. Even the severest punishments under the Divine administration are not oppressive, be-

cause they are not unjust—not inconsistent with infinite holiness, wisdom, and goodness. That an institution is Divine, cannot therefore be made an apology for infringing on the rights of man, or of any other class of beings.

2. The instruction afforded by this law relates to all practical goodness. It supplies the rule for doing whatever man is called to do. It is not an approximation of the right—not a problematical and doubtful rule, which may or may not eventuate in success; but an authoritative and infallible guide to righteousness. The instructive tendency of this law is finely characterized in the following passage: "The law of the Lord is perfect, converting the soul: the testimony of the Lord is sure, making wise the simple. The statutes of the Lord are right, rejoicing the heart: the commandment of the Lord is pure, enlightening the eyes. The fear of the Lord is clean, enduring forever: the judgments of the Lord are true and righteous altogether. More to be desired are they than gold, yea than much fine gold: sweeter also than honey and the honey-comb. Moreover by them is thy servant warned; and in keeping of them is great reward." But the special advantage which this law confers is a knowledge of the invisible state, and of man's duty relating thereto. Its requirements appertain not wholly to this life, but also to that which is to come. Future rewards and punishments, with all their interminable duration and unfathomable mystery, are brought to bear up-

on human conduct. Man is taught not only how to live, but how to live forever.

3. Not less wonderful is this law for the dignity which it confers on humanity. Aside from the Bible, how perfectly brutish is man! He belongs to the soil as much as the trees of the field, and his whole life is spent in catering to the flesh. He has no hope, and is without God in the world. A low round of pleasures and pursuits, purely animal, and often vicious, occupy him till the grave opens to hide his insignificance. How is the scene changed when the law of God is given to such a being! The clod rises to a man—the brute puts on the lineaments of a God. Before, all was bounded by earth and time: now, heaven and eternity are necessary ideas—considerations taken into the account whenever any thing is to be done, or to be left undone. The law of God is, in short, a pledge of extended duration, and of interests in other worlds. All the distressing darkness, and brevity, and poverty, which hang over life, disappear at this authoritative call to obey the mandate of the King Immortal. The present life no longer seems abortive; it is seen as the grand initiative to a still grander life. Death, so fearful and hopeless to those who know not God, under this law becomes a simple and unspeakably gainful transition. It does but bring the christian into the more immediate presence of his great employer, and into that land where the recompense of obedience is fully meted out.

"O 'tis a glorious boon to die!
This favor can't be prized too high."

Much of this firm confidence we owe to the fact, that we are bound by the law of God to an accountability in another world. Obligations are not discharged by death; the grave, all-destroying as it is, cannot destroy the claims of heaven.

Such are the objects of that law by which men ought to be governed, and by which they must be judged. The law, like its author, is open to contempt; it can be vilified, if any choose, but not with impunity; it can be violated, if any dare, but not without death. "The soul that sinneth, it shall die." There is no parade of authority, no display of power, no bugbear terrors to frighten; and yet the doom of the transgressor is as fixed as fate. God is not trifling with men: they must be good—good as his law requires—or perish. Nor is this goodness to be expected somewhere else, or this law more fitting another place. We are to do his will here on earth as it is done in heaven. The law of God is the very best law for this world, and the only law which ensures justice and happiness to mankind.

We are now to turn our attention to Civil Law, as a subordinate agency in carrying out the designs of the Great Lawgiver.

CHAPTER III.

CIVIL GOVERNMENT.

ITS ORIGIN AND DESIGN.

Civil Government was not instituted by Christianity: it is an institution of nature, confirmed and sanctioned by Christianity. Man, in the present condition of his nature, cannot exist in society, without feeling the need of government. He wants security, which he cannot have in the absence of civil law. As this want is common to all men, we find all men inclined to establish and support some kind of governmental regulation, which shall meet the exigencies of their condition. In this view of the subject, government has very much the nature of a voluntary compact. But the actual origin of government is modified by two facts. *First:* The condition of man at the commencement of society, was not such as to admit of a compact. The original pair were the only adults, till their own children had grown up, and all the government possible, under the circumstances, was self-government. On the parents, of course, devolved the duty of governing their offspring, but not by contract—it was a duty growing out of the relation of the parties. Parental government was just as necessary as parental support and care. *Secondly:* All men are at first infants, and enter into society in a state of infancy; it follows, therefore, that they become members of civil society before they have attained to the age in which a choice could be made. Men are born into government—they come under its protection at the moment of their birth; and this has been the case of all who have ever lived, since governments were established. At first, government was only parental, but this, as men increased, gradually gave place to what is called civil government. Monarchies, however, even at this day, are often not essentially different from the first type of government. The king is a chief father, or great parent—a pope—whose will is acknowledged to be supreme, so far as the will of one man may be supreme over that of another.

The further modification of government, by the introduction of written laws, and by a division of governmental powers among many, instead of consolidating them in one individual, is the result of that maturity to which man attains, by education or experience. These modifications are not essential to the existence of government; they are only a means of giving to it greater perfection.

The origin of civil government shows conclusively what must have been its design. Both revelation and nature also concur in asserting that the institution is of a conservative and beneficent character. "Rulers are not a terror to good works, but to the evil. Wilt thou then not be afraid of the power? Do that which is good, and thou shalt have praise of the same. For he is the minister of God to thee for good. But if thou do that which is evil, be afraid; for he beareth not the sword in vain: for he is the minister of God, a revenger to execute wrath upon him that doeth evil." This needs no comment; and were there any necessity, we might support the doctrines of the passage by a great variety of scriptures, all precisely of the same import.

So far as human authority is concerned, the best exposition of the purposes of government is that contained in our own Declaration of Independence, and in the Constitution of these United States:

"We hold these truths to be self-evident: That all men are created equal; that they are endowed by their Creator with certain inalienable rights; that among these are life, liberty, and the pursuit of happiness. That to secure these rights, governments are instituted among men, deriving their just powers from the consent of the governed; that whenever any form of government becomes destructive of these ends, it is the right of the people to alter or abolish it, and to institute a new government, laying its foundation on such principles, and organizing its powers in such form, as to them shall seem most likely to effect their safety and happiness."—*Declaration of Independence.*

"We, the people of the United States, in order to form a more perfect union, establish justice, ensure tranquillity, provide for the common defence, promote the general welfare, and secure the blessings of liberty to ourselves and our posterity, do ordain and establish this constitution for the United States of America."—*Preamble to the Constitution.*

These authorities are amply sufficient to show the benevolent design of human laws, but I shall add a few others.

"All government has the same general end, which is that of preservation."—MONTESQUIEU, *Spirit of Laws: b.* 11, *ch.* 5.

"The Christian religion is a stranger to mere despotic power."—*Ibid.: book* 24, *ch.* 3.

"Considering the Creator only as a being of infinite *power*, he was able unquestionably to have prescribed whatever laws he pleased to his creature, man, however unjust or severe. But as he is a being of infinite *wisdom*, he has laid down only such laws as were founded in those relations of justice, that existed in the nature of things antecedent to any positive precept. These are the eternal, immutable laws of good and evil, to which the Creator himself, in all his dispensations, conforms; and which he has enabled human reason to discover, so far as they are necessary for the conduct of human actions. Such, among others, are these principles: that we should live honestly, should hurt nobody, and should render to every one his due; to which three general precepts Justinian has reduced the whole doctrine of the law."—BLACKSTONE, *Com., Intro.: sec.* 2.

"We ought not, therefore, to separate the science of public law from that of ethics, nor encourage the dangerous suggestion, that governments are not as strictly bound by the obligations of truth, justice, and humanity, in relation to other powers, as they are in the management of their own local concerns."—KENT, *Com.: sec.* 1.

"The divine right of *kings* is, like the divine right of other magistrates—the law of the land, or even actual and quiet possession of their office—a right ratified, we humbly presume, by the Divine approbation, so long as obedience to their authority appears to be necessary or conducive to the common welfare. Princes are ordained of God, by virtue only of that general decree by which he assents, and adds the sanction of his will, to every law of society which promotes his own purpose, the communication of human happiness."—Dr. PALEY, *Mor. and Pol. Phil.: book* 6, *ch.* 4.

"The fundamental principles which are deducible from the law of nature and from Christianity, respecting political affairs, appear to be these: 1. Political power is rightly *possessed* only when it is possessed by the consent of the community. 2. It is rightly *exercised* only when it subserves the welfare of the community. 3. And only when it subserves this purpose by *means* which the moral law permits." —DYMOND, *Principles of Morality: essay* 3, *ch.* 1.

It will not be necessary, I trust, to make further citations, or to adduce other arguments, in support of this general proposition—That civil government is designed for the good of mankind. But if this be the case, it follows, inevitably, that such government is perverted, whenever it becomes oppressive. Taking our stand upon this fundamental truth—the essential and immutable benevolence of the governmental institution—we shall proceed to examine the LIMITATIONS to which it must necessarily be subjected, and the POWERS with which it is legitimately invested.

CHAPTER IV.

LIMITATIONS OF CIVIL GOVERNMENT.

THESE limitations may be stated as follows:

1. Civil government cannot bind the conscience.
2. It cannot impair any other natural rights or powers of mankind.
3. It cannot release man from his responsibility to God.
4. It cannot change the nature of vice and virtue.

SECTION I.

CIVIL GOVERNMENT CANNOT BIND THE CONSCIENCE.

IT has always been the aim of tyrants to invade the conscience. They know if human nature is allowed to possess any rule of duty, superior to that which they prescribe, that obedience will depend very much upon the character of what is required. A good man will not keep a bad law, if he is left to believe that his own conscience should govern his conduct. Hence it becomes necessary to subvert the very framework of the human constitution, to make it subserve the purpose of oppression. Government cannot be made an engine of despotism till it has done violence to the moral system of man. Conscience is that faculty by which we distinguish between right and wrong; it is the moral sense, and essential to the constitution of moral agency. If this natural faculty, which the Creator has fixed in the human soul, is under the control of government, then obedience is due to law, whatever may be its character. Human law becomes the highest law known to man, and all deviations from it are justly punishable. Against this enormous outrage on the rights of man—this utter prostitution of civil authority—it behooves all who value the peace and welfare of society, to enter their solemn protest. The following considerations will place the subject in its true light:

1. It subverts the design of government. We have seen that the institution of law was intended for the benefit, and not for the injury of man; it follows, therefore, that any violence done to the human faculties, is an abuse of governmental powers. The Creator established law to operate in conjunction with conscience, and not irrespective of it; much less did he intend that law should mar his work, by usurping control over the moral faculty.

2. But the thing is physically impossible. Conscience may be destroyed, but it cannot be bound. We may extinguish the light which God has placed in the soul, but we cannot change its nature. All

attempts to bind conscience are, in reality, attempts to annihilate it. The use of the moral faculty is to judge of right and wrong, and it has no other use; hence those who interfere with its decisions, virtually say there shall be no conscience.

3. God himself does not, by any of his laws, invade this faculty. His laws are as precisely adapted to our moral constitution, as the physical world is to our material organism. Light is not more congenial to the eye, nor air to the lungs, than is the moral law of Jehovah to the moral faculty in man.

4. Conscience is an element of our nature, and cannot be subjected to any human authority. Man's conscience is as his eyes, or his hands, or his feet—that is, a part of himself—made such by the Creator, and to disturb its action is to say that man shall not be man. The eyes are left to see, and the ears to hear, because common sense has hitherto kept us from the gross absurdity and injustice of restraining their use. We may legislate against the abuse, but not against the use of these faculties. Law may cooperate with nature in promoting the good of man, and this is all it may do: it can have no power to arrest the design, or to change the plan of nature.

5. As conscience is the faculty which constitutes us moral agents, it follows that law cannot interfere without, at the same time, transferring this moral agency. When the law determines for us, it must release us from all obligation to determine for ourselves. This would be to lodge responsibility in

government, where God has never placed it, and to withhold it from man, who is alone competent to the trust.

6. If the law may control conscience in one thing, it may in another, and so on, till man becomes the merest tool of government, and that, too, without the slightest regard to the moral character of government. A bad action, if commanded, is, upon this hypothesis, just as obligatory as a good one. No right to discriminate can be allowed, except by giving to conscience its legitimate supremacy. Either conscience must be supreme, or man must cease from all distinctions between right and wrong.

These reasons, we think, establish beyond successful contradiction, both the immutability and inviolableness of conscience. Able jurists have, however, conceded that conscience may be bound in two respects. First, in things morally indifferent; and secondly, in things which are morally right, as in this case the civil law has the sanction of the law of God. As to the first of these distinctions, it does not belong to this inquiry, because things morally indifferent—if there be any such things—can have no reference to conscience. The second particular is more important, but obviously fallacious. Human laws, when just, have the same force as Divine, we grant; yet this does not help the matter, for the reason that the Divine law no more binds the conscience, than the air we breathe binds the lungs, or than light binds the eye. Conscience is in harmony with this law, but the law no more binds conscience, than conscience binds the law. The law of God is that standard of perfect rectitude with which man's conscience was made to agree, and the agreement between them is only a natural coincidence: it is not a mastery, not a binding, in the ordinary sense of these terms.

This view of the subject places before us the true relation of man to God's moral government. He is not bound as a slave; his obedience is not servile—exacted with despotic authority. It is the hearty acquiescence of the good in goodness. It is doing as man was made to do, that is, right and only right, forever. Not to do good is the soul's death, because it was created and fitted for this very work, and for none other. Obedience to God is the natural element of man, and harmonizes with all his powers. A pure law is just as essential to the moral constitution as pure air is to the physical constitution. The higher law, then, is conservative, and binds man—if it can be said to bind him at all—only as food binds the stomach, or as the vital air binds the organs of respiration. Conscience responds to this law with infinite pleasure, and from its nature must inevitably repel everything foreign to it. This moral faculty is always in accordance with the Divine law, because that law is always right, and it accords with all other laws, so far as they are right, and no farther.

How presumptuous must it be for man to attempt to bind a power which God cannot bind! He respects his own work, and legislates in accordance with the faculties he has made; but man legislates as he pleases, and then vainly endeavors to conform nature to his futile and wicked laws. Such lawgivers would not hesitate to chastise the sea to make it obey them, and they would be quite as wisely employed as they are in laying commands upon conscience.

SECTION II.

CIVIL GOVERNMENT CANNOT IMPAIR ANY OF THE NATURAL RIGHTS OR POWERS OF MANKIND.

It is not necessary to go into an enumeration of the rights or powers of man, in order to perceive their true relation to civil law. The summary statement of them in the Declaration of Independence—"life, liberty, and the pursuit of happiness"—is quite sufficient. They all stand on the same basis, and if one falls, the rest cannot stand. The right to life is no more a right than any other endowment of man. It is neither more sacred, nor more inalienable, than the right to liberty. Nor is the right to liberty more under the control of law, than the right to see, or to eat, or to walk. These last, with various others that might be named, are, like life and liberty, conditions of being. We have them from God when we have existence, and so long as existence remains these rights must remain, unless taken away by Him who gave them.

Why some of these rights are taken away by legislation, and others not, can only be accounted for by the weakness of man. He has never been able, in the utmost stretch of his tyranny, to quite subvert the entire endowments of his race. He treats his fellow, however, as the robber treats the victim of his plunder—that is, strips him of whatever is most available, and lets him go. The slave must be allowed life, as that is not a transferable commodity, and cannot be seized upon by his master; but he must give up liberty and the pursuit of happiness, for these have a marketable value.

That human laws have no rightful power over the constitutional endowments of man's nature, is a truth recognized by the ablest jurists. So obvious indeed is this fact, that Blackstone says, the civil law can neither take them away, nor by giving them its sanction, add any thing to the authority by which we hold them. They are just as much ours without, as with legislation—that is to say, they are wholly beyond the reach of any law that man can make.

"Those rights which God and nature have established, and are therefore called natural rights, such as are life and liberty, need not the aid of human laws to be more effectually invested in every man than they are; neither do they receive any additional strength, when declared by the municipial laws to be inviolable. On the contrary, no human legislature has power to abridge or destroy them, unless the owner shall himself commit some act that amounts to a forfeiture." *Com., Intro.: sec.* 2.

Man can no more change these God-given rights of humanity, than he can change the seasons, or reverse the laws of physical existence. He may affect to control them, and so he may affect to control the winds and tides, but in neither case would the attempt deserve serious consideration. This is fully declared by the same high authority to which I have just referred.

"The law of nature, being coeval with mankind, and dictated by God himself, is of course superior in obligation to any other. It is binding over all the globe, in all countries, and at all times; no human laws are of any validity, if contrary to this; and such of them as are valid derive all their force, and all their authority mediately or immediately, from this original." *Com.: sec.* 2.

We may go yet farther, and affirm with Dr. Cudworth, that even God himself cannot force man to obey an unrighteous law.

"We see, then, that it is so far from being true, that all moral good and evil, just and unjust, (if they be anything,) are made by mere will and arbitrary commands, (as many conceive,) that it is not possible that any command of God or man should oblige, otherwise than by virtue of that which is naturally just. And though particular promises and commands be made by will, yet it is not will, but nature, that obligeth to the doing of things promised or commanded, or makes them such things as ought to be done. For mere will cannot change the moral nature of actions, nor the nature of intellectual beings. And, therefore, if there were no natural justice, that is, if the rational or intellectual nature in itself were indetermined and unobliged to any thing, and so destitute of all morality, it were not possible that any thing should be made morally good or evil, obligatory or unlawful, or that any moral obligation should be begotten by any will or command whatsoever." *Concerning Eternal and Immutable Morality: book* 1, *chap.* 2.

If any object to this position, let them remember that God cannot be unjust, and that it is, therefore, impossible for him to command what is not just.

Hence the idea of his requiring obedience to an unrighteous law, is merely assumed—no such event is possible, but if it were, the result is correctly stated above.

We obey every law of God, because his immutable wisdom and goodness assure us, that he cannot require what is not right. His perfections render it safe to follow him implicitly, whether we comprehend or not the character of his commands. Such assurance, however, we cannot have in reference to any other commands. Man has a fallible or imperfect goodness; God has an infallible or perfect goodness: therefore we obey the latter always, and the former when virtue will permit. Man must either arrogate to himself the perfections of

God, or dismiss all claims to unconditional obedience. The higher law is an emanation from the higher nature, and from that only. This higher nature, be it remembered, is the ample guaranty of integrity and wisdom in all the laws which it imposes. We submit cheerfully to its requirements, because we cannot distrust the source from which they proceed. We know that God is competent to do whatever he will, and that he cannot will that which is not for the best.

It is here that human legislation fails. In forgetfulness of its own incompetency to change the laws of nature, it presumes to deal freely with the constitutional and inalienable rights of mankind. It takes from one and gives to another, as though it were charged with revising the Creator's work. This utter heedlessness of its true province has made human government too frequently a curse instead of a blessing. The evil, however, is not in the institution, but in its abuse. Man has usurped the Divine prerogative—that of determining constitutional rights—and consequently the distribution is unequal. By nature, all are equal in fundamental immunities, but society interferes, with its impious law, and defeats this benevolent arrangement, by making one man a slave, and another his master. All this is done in mere wantonness of power, as no crime is pretended, and no necessity alleged. Rights are taken away from some, because they can be taken away, and they are bestowed on others for the same reason. The cause of such perversions of civil authority, is substantially the same that has led to every other species of human wickedness —an evil heart. From this corrupt fountain have proceeded forth, in all ages, not only murders, thefts, and adulteries, but oppressions and tyrannies of every sort.

SECTION III.

CIVIL GOVERNMENT CANNOT RELEASE MAN FROM HIS RESPONSIBILITY TO GOD.

THE following, among many other reasons, are decisive on this point:

1. Civil government is itself subject to the Divine law. "The powers that be are ordained of God," and are therefore responsible to him. This could not be otherwise, unless on the monstrous supposition of atheism—that there is no God. In this case there would be no power above civil rulers, and the practical effect would be the same as if government were not subject to Divine authority, though in such circumstances the exemption would not affect government alone; it would release subjects as well as rulers from all religious obligations. We should then have only the accident of power as the basis of human laws, and any one might

disregard them without incurring guilt. There would be no fear of God to restrain—no hope of heaven to reward. All motives to obedience would be cut off, except those which flow from temporal considerations.

But civil government has its origin in the Divine law, not barely from a simple decree to that effect. The institution rests upon much more than a statutory basis. It has the relation of an effect to its cause. If we take away from human laws the support which they derive from religion, their stability and usefulness are at an end: the foundation is sapped, and the social fabric precipitated into ruin.

"As the religion of an oath is a necessary vinculum of civil society; so obligation in conscience, respecting the Deity as its original, and as the punisher of the violation thereof, is the very foundation of all civil sovereignty; for pacts and covenants, (into which some would resolve all civil power,) without this obligation in conscience, are nothing but mere words and breath; and the laws and commands of civil sovereigns do not make obligation, but pre-suppose it, as a thing in order of nature before them, and without which they would be invalid."—Dr. CUDWORTH, *Intellectual System: vol. 2, p.* 111.

We have shown that no command of man is binding when opposed to the law of God, hence it follows that the laws of men are utterly incapable of releasing us in any measure from the claims of the higher law. How much stronger is the argument, then, when we add to this the fact, that human government is itself subject in all things to this very law! How can it release others, when it cannot even release itself?

2. But this is further evident from the condition of all legislators and rulers. Men never lose their individuality. Though in authority, they are still but men, and act as men. It is not as legislators or governors only that they are known to God. There are no mere officers. The functions of government are joined to the other responsibilities of individual and personal character. They are duties which men perform as individuals, and for which they are held responsible, precisely as they are for other duties. It is said that "kings can do no wrong," but God does not say it, neither will he judge them as kings, but as men. The acts of a government are acts of individuals—of individual men, whose accountability is in no respect changed by their official character. The delusion, therefore, that civil duties carry with them exemption from religious obligations, is most unfounded. There is no reason why office or power of this kind should have any effect, that will not apply just as well to any other office or power. The president and directors of a bank, or of a manufacturing company, might, with equal propriety, attempt to set aside the Divine law. We admit that civil government is, in some respects, more important than the institutions just named; but this only enhances the obli-

gation of those who administer it, towards Him "by whom kings rule and princes decree justice."

3. Another truth of great weight on this subject is, that civil officers, even the highest of them, are the servants of the people. This is a doctrine recognized, not only in our own country, but where-ever civil liberty is known. With the people is sovereignty, so far as it may rightfully be anywhere among men; and their rulers are their servants. These govermental servants are employed as the police of the body politic. Their services are demanded, on the same principle that we employ the services of other men—that is, because they are beneficial. The physician, the lawyer, or the mechanic, is not more a servant of the public, nor a servant of the public for any other reason than the legislator or the governor. The idea that these servants of the people have power to cancel the law of God, is exceedingly ridiculous. Had not kings, and others entrusted with the duties of government, entered into a conspiracy against the rights of mankind, so great an absurdity would either never have been known, or been known only as an odious usurpation.

If rulers have any power to release us from the Divine law, they have it from those who employ them—that is, the governed give their governors authority to cancel such obligations. The act of release is, then, not the act of governors, but of the people whom they govern. It cannot be otherwise, for "governments derive their just powers from the consent of the governed," and if the people are released from the higher law, they are self-released. It is their own act, and they alone are responsible.

4. It gives to man a power which, as we have shown, God does not possess. God cannot enact an unrighteous law; he cannot, therefore, require obedience to such a law. In other words, he cannot release his creatures from the obligation of justice, and at the same time exercise government over them. But if human legislation is supreme, justice may be set aside, and man may be compelled to obey an unjust law. And if justice may be set aside in one instance, it may in many—in all instances. Thus, on this hypothesis, justice might be banished from the world, and that, too, by the authority of God. Most, it is true, who claim unconditional supremacy for civil law, are atheists; but men professing religion have asserted this horrid doctrine, and quoted scripture to justify it. Surely, they could not have seen its consequences, or they would never have given it countenance.

5. A government having power to dispense with the eternal principles of justice, established by the Creator, and wrought into the human constitution, would be the most terrific engine of oppression that can be conceived. Satanic malice could invent nothing worse. It would be a mockery of God—undoing at will all he has done, and trampling with impunity upon the moral sense of all his creatures.

Such a fearful power—such a diabolical institution, we may be certain has no existence, save among the traitorous imaginings of willful tyrants and their obsequious dupes.

6. The doctrine of a future judgment, or of any judgment whatever, on the part of God, is rendered impossible. If men are under no higher obligations than to human government, they of course have nothing to fear beyond this life, and nothing in this life, except the civil law. It matters not what we call this monstrous perversion; it may bear the outward stamp of atheism or of deism or of Christianity, but it is essentially anti-Christian, and worthy only of our deepest abhorrence.

SECTION IV.

CIVIL GOVERNMENT CANNOT CHANGE THE NATURE OF VICE AND VIRTUE.

There is an immutable distinction between right and wrong, which no human power can subvert. This fixed character of virtue, and its opposite, is one of the most effectual barriers to the progress of tyranny. Could the wicked who bear rule, by any means change the nature of things, then their decretals, however inimical to man or his Maker, might put on the garb of virtue, and challenge the respect of mankind. But no such deception is possible. Vice must appear as vice; it must act on the world as vice, and as vice be detested and spurned by all the human race. The heart of man can form no alliance with it — none, at least, till conscience has ceased to perform its functions—nor can even the intellectual powers be made to approve it. Unschooled and unprompted, we instantly repel it in its grosser kinds, as the baleful destroyer of our happiness. Pope's well known lines are to the point:

> "Vice is a monster of such hateful mien,
> That to be hated, needs but to be seen."

The same is true of virtue. It is an essential and indestructible principle. We approve it intuitively, and covet it as our best good. The very hatred of vice implies an opposite, which we love. Virtue is so interwoven with our nature, and so congenial to its interests, that it is approved by those who do not practice it.

The impotence of human power, when directed against virtue itself, is well expressed by Dr. Brown:

"A sovereign, it has been truly said, may enact and rescind laws, but he cannot create or annihilate a single virtue. It might be amusing to consider, not one sovereign only, but all the sovereigns of the different nations of the earth, endeavoring to change a virtue into a vice — a vice into a virtue. If an imperial enactment of a senate of kings were to declare, that it was in future to be a crime for a mother to love her child — for a child to venerate his parent — if high privileges were to be attached to the most ungrateful, and an act of gratitude to a benefactor declared to be a capital offence — would the heart of man obey this impotent legislation? Would remorse and self approbation vary with the command of man, or of any number of men? And would he, who, notwithstanding these laws, had obstinately persisted in the illegality of loving his parent, or his benefactor, tremble to meet his own conscience with the horror which the parricide feels? There is, indeed, a power by which 'princes decree justice;' but it is a power above the mere voice of kings — a power which has previously fixed in the breasts of those who receive the decree, a love of the very virtue which kings, even when kings are most virtuous, can only enforce. And it is well for man, that the feeble authorities of this earth cannot change the sentiments of our hearts with the same facility as they can throw fetters on our hands. There would then, indeed, be no hope to the oppressed. The greater the oppression, the stronger motive would there be to make obedience to oppression a virtue, and every species of guilt, which the powerful might love to exercise, amiable in the eyes of the miserable victims. All virtue, in such circumstances, would soon perish from the earth. A single tyrant would be sufficient to destroy, what all the tyrants that have ever disgraced this moral scene, have been incapable of extinguishing — the remorse which was felt in the bosom of him who could order every thing but vice and virtue — and the scorn, and the sorrow, and the wrath, of every noble heart, in the contemplation of his guilty power.

"Nature has not thrown us upon the world with such feeble principles as these. She has given us virtues of which no power can deprive us, and has fixed in the soul of him whom more than fifty nations obey, a restraint on his power, from which the servile obedience of all the nations on the globe could not absolve him. There may be flatterers to surround a tyrant's throne, with knees ever ready to bow on the very blood with which his steps are stained, and with voices ever ready to applaud the guilt that has been already perpetrated, and to praise, even with a sort of prophetic quickness of discernment, the cruelties in prospect which they only anticipate. There may be servile warriors, to whom it is indifferent whether they succor or oppress, whether they enslave or free, if they have only drowned in blood, with sufficient promptness, the thousands of human beings whom they have been commanded to sweep from the earth. There may be statesmen as servile, to whom the people are nothing, and to whom every thing is dear, but liberty and virtue. These eager emulators of each other's baseness, may sound forever in the ears of him on whose vices their own power depends, that what he has willed *must* be right, because he has willed it—and priests still more base, from the very dignity of that station which they dishonor, not content with proclaiming that crimes are right, may add their consecrating voice, and proclaim that they are holy, because they are deeds of a vicegerent of that Holiness which is supreme. But the flatteries, which only sound in the ear, or play, perhaps, with feeble comfort around the surface of the heart, are unable to reach that deeper-seated sense of guilt within."—*Philosophy of the Human Mind: lect.* 75.

The changeless nature of moral principle, and the necessity which it throws upon legislation, of conforming its character to the moral law, are the bulwark of human rights. When government deviates from the standard of rectitude, it produces ruin, and all the forces of nature engage against it, or, rather, for its restoration to purity. As the result of this conservatism, which nature always exerts, government grows weaker as it grows vicious, until it becomes too vicious to be endured, and then it is overthrown. This is the origin of most revolutions. That there have been instances of the exact reverse — of good governments overthrown by national degeneracy — does not weaken the argument, but strengthens it, rather; showing that the governmental institution must conform to the moral condition of those among whom it exists. It is not pretended that the moral principle is always equally well developed in communities, or that people are, by any means, incorruptible. Private citizens, as well as public functionaries, nations as well as individuals, may become depraved; but this does not prove that virtue itself is corruptible. It only proves that men may depart from virtue.

This immutable distinction between vice and virtue is, in fact, the only basis of character and of law. If good and evil were the same, or convertible into each other, courts of equity could not exist, nor could there be any foundation for rewards or punishments, since it would make no difference whether people did right or wrong. All law is of necessity based upon this pre-existing and ineradicable difference in the nature of things, and to subvert it is as impossible as it would be to change the order of the universe.

CHAPTER V.

THE POWERS OF CIVIL GOVERNMENT.

As might be expected, these powers are exactly the opposite of the propositions contained in the foregoing chapter. They may be stated thus:

1. Civil government can maintain the rights of conscience.
2. It can maintain the other natural rights and powers of mankind.
3. It can enforce obedience to the law of God.
4. It can maintain the immutable distinction between vice and virtue.

SECTION I.

CIVIL GOVERNMENT CAN MAINTAIN THE RIGHTS OF CONSCIENCE.

The end of government is conservation—not the conservation of itself, as too many suppose, but the conservation of the rights of the people who live under it. The happiness of mankind depends very much upon their adherence to that standard of moral rectitude which God has established in their own consciences, and in his holy word. To do right is a privilege no less than a duty. Man, being constituted as he is, could not have laid upon him a heavier infliction than to be obliged to do wrong. It would be a perpetual crucifixion of himself, so long as any sense of moral obligation, or any perception of the excellence of virtue, and the loathsomeness of vice, remained to him. Ixion, chained to his wheel, had a more tolerable fate. Such an one might truly say, "O wretched man that I am! who shall deliver me from the body of this death?" To take away all vice, and all tendency to vice, and thereby bring in the blessings of everlasting righteousness, were the great objects of redemption—that higher and most wonderful act of the Divine government. Human laws, at best, fall very far short of attempting complete moral excellence. For the fullness of virtue we must depend on God—on the higher law—while to man, as a co-worker, is left the regulation and guardianship of character, in a few subordinate particulars. We may derive comfort from the fires kindled in our dwellings, but it is not possible for artificial fires to supply the place of the sun: they are convenient and useful, but altogether incapable of meeting the wants of physical existence. So government may do something towards conserving the morals of the world, but our main dependence must be upon a higher power.

In protecting the exercise of conscience, civil government is co-operative with the higher law. And this is its province always. It may contribute to the assistance and perfection of natural endowments, but not to their destruction or perversion. Like the daily labor of man, by which he aids the productiveness of nature, and thereby gains a better subsistence, government enhances—if it be not misdirected—that good order in society which nature designed, but which, owing to human depravity, is too little prevalent, without the aid of civil authority. The law not only prohibits all injury of the moral faculty, but stimulates its activity, by exacting the fulfillment of equitable obligations. If men do not pay honest debts, provision is made for the forcible seizure and sale of enough of their effects to liquidate the demand, and satisfy the claims of justice.

SECTION II.

CIVIL GOVERNMENT CAN MAINTAIN THE NATURAL RIGHTS AND POWERS OF MANKIND.

We might have included, without impropriety, under this head, what we have advanced in the foregoing section, as conscience is unquestionably one of our natural powers, and the right to use it, one of our natural rights. But the transcendent importance of the moral faculty, in all discussions of this nature, renders it desirable to give greater prominence to its claims, than could be done in a hasty sketch, where many particulars were grouped together. Conscience is not only a natural power, the exercise of which is guarantied to us by the same principle that ensures us the use of our hands and feet, our eyes and ears, but it is a part of man, vastly higher in its character—so much higher, that without it, right and wrong could not be affirmed of man: he would have no moral character whatever—he would not be man. While civil government is charged with guarding this fountain of good and evil, it is also charged with preserving all the various subordinate natural rights of men. These I need not name in detail. They include everything bestowed by Creative goodness: the right to be, to be human beings, to provide for all our wants, to use and enjoy all our faculties and powers; and if there be any other conceivable right, imparted by the Creator, which may come within the province of human guardianship, it is provided for and conserved by the civil law.

For the maintenance of these rights, government was instituted. It has no other purpose with regard to them. Destroy them it certainly cannot, without the most willful and wicked perversion of its nature.

As there is strength in union, by the coalition of men for the common defence, a power is brought into existence for securing public order and individual rights, which must otherwise have remained unknown. One man, however wise or powerful, cannot protect himself against all other men; he might be injured or destroyed, in ways too numerous to mention, if compelled to be his own protector. But by entering into the general confederacy for maintaining the rights of man, he gains protection with very little trouble. Just as a man can cross a bridge by paying a trifling toll, whereas he would be wholly unable to build a bridge for his own accommodation. So with public roads, and almost all other things of a public nature—all professions, trades, and business pursuits, except so far as they minister directly to the personal wants of those who pursue them, are based upon the same principle. They are possible, because many share in them, and are benefited by them. Physicians, lawyers, and mechanics are sustained by the many—that is, by the public. No individual would be able to meet the expense of such assistance, if he must purchase the entire of a professional man's services, in order to have his services at all. But as many are in like circumstances with himself, their common want renders it possible, by a division of his labors, for each one to have all he needs, and at a moderate expense. Thus is it with government. If the task of self-protection was thrown upon each one, apart from this arrangement, it would be wholly impossible, because one man has not the strength of a hundred, or a thousand, or a million. In the confederacy—that is, under civil government—he, in effect, increases his own powers indefinitely; and it is the only way he can increase them, except by science. Knowledge is power, but it is not in all cases equivalent to the power of coalition.

This tremendous engine—public authority—being instituted solely for the good of society, should be employed for no other purpose than to keep the rights and immunities of such society intact. If diverted from its original design, and made to operate, with all its crushing power, in favor of itself, or of any particular member in society, to the exclusion of others, nothing can do greater mischief. In such case, either society, as a whole, becomes the victim of its own institution, or the injury falls upon some particular class of persons, who are thereby stripped of their rights, and ruined by what should have been their inviolable protection.

To cut off from equal privileges, whole races of men, under the pretext of government, is robbery, perpetrated in the name of order—the rankest injustice, committed in the name of justice. It is in politics as it would be in medicine, if the physician should give fatal poisons where he ought to give only salutary remedies. The higher law of nature, and of nature's God, on which the civil law is founded, has made the essential rights of men inalienable;

and though they may be obstructed, they can never be destroyed. So far as conscience is concerned, the unjust law is, in fact, no law, and should be treated as a nullity, because it is unjust. But justice and power are not always combined, and hence that may pass as law, and be enforced as law, which merits only detestation. Of this character are all governments not strictly conformed to the law of God; but perversion has its limits, and wicked governments can only make impotent attempts against the constitution of things. They may strip a man of his rights by an unrighteous decree, but their decree is null and void before God. The higher law—the law of the universe—the law of the uncreated God—shall stand, in spite of any adverse legislation on the part of his creatures. What that law gives belongs to those to whom it is given, until the law which gave it shall take it away. Man can take away property, but he cannot take away rights; he can take away life, but not the right to life.

SECTION III.

CIVIL GOVERNMENT CAN ENFORCE OBEDIENCE TO THE LAW OF GOD.

We have already virtually affirmed as much as is contained in this proposition, but to complete the illustration of the principles laid down, it is necessary to vary their application. Conscience, and all other natural powers and rights of humanity, are, in the fullest sense of the term, laws of God. They embody his will, and constitute unalterable conditions of being and of happiness. The maintenance and enforcement of these — the avowed object of all just government — is to enforce obedience to the Divine law. But these natural laws have a special interpretation, which is also to be enforced by the civil law. The Scriptures establish government, not merely for the sake of conserving those few obvious rights which are indispensable to the bare existence of civil society, but for the securing, as far as may be, of that moral excellence which is essential to eternal life. That revelation has, at least, co-ordinate authority with nature, as a foundation of civil government, is very clearly stated by Blackstone:

> "Providence, in compassion to the frailty, the imperfection, and the blindness of human reason, hath been pleased, at sundry times and in divers manners, to discover and enforce its laws by an immediate and direct revelation. The doctrines thus delivered, we call the revealed or Divine law, and they are to be found only in the Holy Scriptures. These precepts, when revealed, are found, upon comparison, to be really a part of the original law of nature, as they tend, in all their consequences, to man's felicity. But we are not thence to conclude that the knowledge of these truths was attainable by reason, in its present corrupted state; since we find that, until they were revealed, they were hid from the wisdom of ages. As, then, the moral precepts of this law are indeed of the same original with those of the law of

nature, so their intrinsic obligation is of equal strength and perpetuity. Yet, undoubtedly, the revealed law has infinitely more authenticity than that moral system which is framed by ethical writers, and denominated the natural law; because one is the law of nature, expressly declared so to be by God himself; the other is only what, by the assistance of human reason, we imagine to be such. If we could be as certain of the latter as we are of the former, both would have an equal authority; but, till then, they can never be put in any competition together."—*Com., Intro.: sec.* 2.

The Bible says, "Thou shalt not kill;" and this command, it will not be denied, is entirely consonant with the dictates of natural justice; we, therefore, in prohibiting murder, are compelling obedience to the Bible; and that, too, in accordance with the most enlightened principles of legislation. It is not pretended that all the duties enjoined by the law of God come within the cognizance of civil law. Both nature and revelation teach many things that cannot be made the subject of legislation, because men have not the wisdom necessary to make or administer laws in relation to these duties. Nor are such laws absolutely essential to the existence of civil society, the maintenance of which is the great object of human government.

Another reason for this limitation of political authority is, that the government of God depends not altogether upon man for the execution of its laws. Offences against nature are always partly punished by nature, and where such offences are not against society, the laws of society have nothing to do with them, and their correction should be left entirely to nature. It is the province of the higher law to enforce its own sanctions, whether of punishment or reward, but it may employ, for this purpose, within certain limits, or, in other words, as far as the good order of society demands, the subordinate agency of human government.

But the power of civil law, to enforce the requirements of the Divine law, rests chiefly on its relation to the latter. The Divine law is supreme, and it is not possible that a subordinate law, or the law of a subordinate power, should be rightfully at variance with that which is above it. Hence, in this confederacy, the laws of a state are considered null when they are not conformed to the constitution of the United States, and, in like manner, all enactments of Congress and of state legislatures, are void, if not in accordance with the constitutions to which these legislative bodies severally owe their existence. In every thing requisite, the lower law is bound to sustain the higher—the authority derived, that from which it is derived. This must be especially true in the case before us, because the higher law commands all right, and prohibits all wrong; so that the law of man, unless perverted, is, of necessity promotive of the Divine law.

SECTION IV.

CIVIL GOVERNMENT CAN MAINTAIN THE IMMUTABLE DISTINCTION BETWEEN VICE AND VIRTUE.

The distinction between vice and virtue is so fixed and immutable, that it can neither be created nor destroyed by human authority; but still, a power which can neither create nor destroy, may subserve other purposes, equally important to the social system. The lexicographer does not originate words, or their meanings, and yet his labors are useful. By collecting words and their meanings, as they exist, he becomes a convenient, though not an infallible exponent of the language. So the civil code may be allowed to represent justice, as established by the Creator. But with the legislator, as with the lexicographer, there is no infallibility; either may err, and erring, may pervert the truth, instead of maintaining it. Nor is there any security against evils of this kind, except the strength of those inherent principles, which are outraged by such infractions. A bad law will be nearly or quite inoperative among a good people, for the same reason that a blundering, imperfect book is contemned by the intelligent—namely, deficiency of character. Such a law, not having the qualities demanded by an upright people, would be instinctively rejected as a nuisance. It would not promote the object of legislation, and could not be endured without great affliction. Law is acceptable among the virtuous, just in proportion to its goodness—that is, just in proportion as it is adapted to promote virtue and suppress vice. It has ever been the professed object of legislation to attain this end, and all nations, of every age, have attempted to fix their civil regulations upon what to them appeared to be the dictates of justice. The following description of law, which Mr. Chitty pronounces the "most perfect that can either be found or conceived," was given by Demosthenes, and shows conclusively, what were the views of mankind in the earliest ages:

> "The design and object of laws is, to ascertain what is just, honorable, and expedient; and when that is discovered, it is proclaimed as a general ordinance, equal and impartial to all. This is the origin of law, which, for various reasons, all are under obligation to obey, but especially because all law is the invention and gift of heaven, the sentiment of wise men, the correction of every offence, and the general compact of the state; to live in conformity with which is the duty of every individual in society."—*Orat.* 1, *cont. Aristogit.*

The fact seems to be, that human law is an instrumentality, which the Great Lawgiver uses to further the execution of his own eternal statutes. Many of these statutes are so profound, that the formal agency of man cannot be employed in giving them effect; but there are others more palpable, and to aid in the maintenance of such, civil law was instituted. Hence, it is the object of our laws every where, to condemn what the reason and conscience of mankind condemn, and to uphold what reason and conscience approve. The laws are only a written embodiment of the public mind on the subject of morals—of morals as they appertain to the most common and tangible rights of human beings. The people—created to feel the need of justice and protection—express, in the form of written laws, their sense of these things, and make the declaration of principles a rule of action. Such is civil law. In nothing either more or less than an effort to promote virtue, and to prevent or punish vice, in accordance with nature and the word of God.

Government has this power of co-operation in support of right, on the same ground that man, and all other creatures, have power to live according to the constitution that God has given them. And the whole design of the institution is to ensure conformity to the higher law, which he has thus interwoven with their very nature, as well as amplified and reaffirmed in his holy word. In this, its true light, civil government appears as a divinely appointed means of accomplishing the good order essential to the happiness of society. It is emphatically a Divine institution, and when conducted as it should be, has the sanction of the Most High. This agrees with the explicit language of scripture, "Submit yourselves to every ordinance of man for the Lord's sake: whether it be to the king as supreme; or unto governors, as unto those that are sent by him for the punishment of evil doers, and for the praise of them that do well." The duty of submission, is here enforced with all those qualifications which ever pertain to the supremacy of conscience. It is only while kings and governors rule as they should, that we are to submit to them for the Lord's sake. They have authority, and have it from him, but it is only authority to do right. He releases none of his creatures from their obligations to him, nor gives any the right to require of them what he would not.

CHAPTER VI.

OBEDIENCE TO CIVIL GOVERNMENT.

From the preceding chapters, it will very readily be inferred, that obedience to civil law is a duty, in all cases, when the law is what it should be. A right law, though made by man, is, to all intents and purposes, a law of God; because it is sanctioned by him, and may even be said to have been made at his command. But it must be kept in mind, that the duty of obedience depends entirely on the character of the law. God, who is the fountain of all legislative power, gives no authority to make a bad law—that is to say, he gives no authority to subvert his own laws, which are all good. If bad laws were obligatory, then the Divine law might be nullified by wicked men, whenever they chose, and society, released from all obligation to heaven, would be under the necessity of plunging into the depths of wickedness, at the bidding of government. Whether or not the Most High has, in this way, left the claims of his own law contingent, is a question too plain for argument. It supposes that the inferior authority can annihilate the superior: or, in other words, that the decree of man can set aside the decree of God. Such a result would be the reverse of all established ideas among men, and contrary to all known possibilities in the nature of things. The supremacy of God is not conditional, but unconditional; and the supremacy of his law is not mutable, but immutable. And yet, on an imagined necessity of conforming to the requirements of human law, whether right or wrong, has been based every tyrannical government that has cursed the world. Perceiving that they had a right to do some things, rulers and law-makers have presumed to do whatever they pleased; and had the extreme audacity to claim Divine authority for all their enormous wickedness, as well as for their most innocent and useful acts. They have forgotten that law-makers are always under law to God, and that law itself must be lawful, in order to have authority.

It is well known that in all human legislation, whenever there is a conflict in the laws, the higher authority controls the lower. The law of a single state never sets aside a law of the confederacy to which that state belongs; nor can a legislative enactment subvert the constitution, from which such legislature derives its power. Hence, all analogy, and all history, as well as all reason, are against this absurd pretension of wicked men, who claim for human laws that infallibility and supremacy which belong only to Almighty God.

Notwithstanding no reason can be given for this foolish and barefaced usurpation of authority, most governments continue to maintain it. It is true, there are moments of relaxation, in which a sort of political toleration prevails, but ever and anon this old intolerance springs up—showing that its temporary suspension was accidental, and that the essential principles of human freedom are not yet well understood, except by a very few. Whenever occasion offers, almost every government is ready to insist upon the fullest obedience, without any reference to principles of rectitude. The performance of some contract, or the carrying out of a compromise, or the maintenance of some ancient usage, is considered a valid reason for enforcing law to the uttermost. It may be, that the object proposed by the law, ranks among the darkest of crimes, yet this, according to the theory under consideration, does not absolve the subject: the state must judge for him in matters of morality, and his conscience must be committed to public keeping. This at once destroys all individual responsibility, and makes the state, or its officers, answerable for the guilt of obedience to wicked laws. But Christians, well knowing that such an excuse could never avail them, have uniformly contemned the laws of men, whenever such laws could not be kept without violating the law of God. Here has been the battle ground of the saints in all ages. The several persecutions through which the church has passed, have all taken their rise at this point. The authority of heaven and earth, having come into conflict, believers have had to "choose whom they would serve." No one in the least acquainted with the Bible, or with church history, will need any confirmation of this statement. We may, however, refer to one instance, in which the conflict of authority was so direct as to admit of no possible mistake, and the approval of the act of disobedience so immediately manifest, as to leave no doubt. The three worthies who were cast into the fire by the king of Babylon, had every assurance of the will of their earthly sovereign, and that will was to them the highest of human laws, yet, because of its palpable contrariety to the will of God, they deliberately and repeatedly disobeyed it. Other instances, of a similar kind, are frequent in both the Old and New Testaments. But in the vast majority of instances, where believers have been called to suffer for obeying God rather than man, their recompense has been defered to "the resurrection of the just." No miraculous deliverance awaited them, nor did they expect any; they were contented to leave the time, and the measure of their reward, to Him who had called them "to glory and virtue."

It is evident, that religion could not exist on the earth, if God had given to man such authority as our politicians claim. For a law might at any time be made, prohibiting the worship of Jehovah, and abolishing any or all other of his laws. Such pretensions are therefore openly hostile to Christianity. Religion cannot co-exist with them, nor they with it.

But, before leaving this part of our subject, it may be well to notice yet further, on whom rests the responsibility of deciding the question of obedience. It is the individual, ever. Each human being must decide for himself. God deals with men simply; he knows nothing of transferred obligations, or of corporate responsibilities. Dr. Paley, though generally too much inclined to the doctrine of expediency, on moral and political questions, is very explicit here. Speaking of the duty of resistance, he says:

> "But who shall judge this? We answer, every man for himself. In contentions between the sovereign and the subject, the parties acknowledge no common arbitrator; and it would be absurd to refer the decision to those whose conduct has provoked the question, and whose own interest, authority, and fate, are immediately concerned in it.—*Mor. and Pol. Phil: book* 5, *ch.* 3.

Indeed, without this right, no man could maintain even his own life, or his rationality, to say nothing of his virtue. For the civil law might command him to kill himself, or to destroy his mental faculties, and his advisers might concur with the law in this abominable requisition: so that if the decision was made dependent upon any other than the individual himself, there would be no security.

CHAPTER VII.

IMPROVEMENTS IN CIVIL GOVERNMENT.

To all who survey the history of mankind, it must appear remarkable that governmental reforms have so seldom been conducted in a peaceful and happy manner. They have generally been occasions not only of violence and bloodshed, but of every sort of injustice and extravagance. Rulers have contended for the full measure of power, with which custom or accident had invested them; and the people, as if doomed to perpetual vassalage, have struggled through disastrous wars, to achieve a modicum of liberty.

This unhappy state of things is as needless as it is irrational. To amend a government, should be as easy as to mend a road, or to repair a piece of machinery. As government originates with the people, they should assume its correction, whenever and wherever there is the least necessity. Its correction is their work, and they should enter upon it freely at all times. To charge them with insurrectionary and seditious designs, when they only propose wholsome changes in civil polity, is the basest treachery. It was probably for this reason, that in most of our state governments, the right of the people peaceably to assemble and petition for a redress of grievances, is especially recognized in the constitution. But the right extends much farther than that of mere petition. The people, as proprietors of government, have full power to introduce changes without the formality of petitioning. And in too many instances, they have relied on the efficacy of supplications, when they should have resorted to more certain measures. If rulers are servants, then the case is clear. Servants may be petitioned, but the more common and more appropriate method is to instruct. The cause of despotism lies, no doubt, in human depravity; but its proximate cause is ignorance and want of concert among the people. Rulers have no power in themselves, and can do nothing, except as they draw to their aid those who are disposed to uphold them. An army, well paid, flattered with titles, and supplied with the munitions of war, is the chief dependence of all despots. And, united with the other causes just named—that is, with ignorance and distraction among the populace—this single means has hitherto been found sufficient to enslave most of the nations of the earth, through every period of their history.

The remedy is easily suggested. Let men use their reason. Let them act as rational beings, and not as "brute beasts, made to be" oppressed—or "destroyed," if they resist oppression. Hitherto, there has been so little concert in action, that tyrants have found it no difficult matter to enslave those from whom they derived all their power. By dividing the people, and making them oppose each other, they have banished liberty and perpetuated despotism, from age to age. And governments, thus perverted have become engines of oppression to the very people who gave them existence, and who alone are interested in their success. Such a perversion, is both unnatural and unnecessary. Civil government was not designed as an infliction—as a judgment: it is not something which the people are predestinated to endure, however vicious it may become; but it is a beneficent institution, originating in the wants of society, and always subject to such modifications as will render it in the highest degree useful. The spirit of these remarks is embraced in that admirable extract, already quoted, from the Declaration of Independence:

> "Whenever any form of government becomes destructive of these ends, [namely, 'life, liberty, and the pursuit of happiness,'] it is the right of the people to alter or abolish it, and to institute a new government, laying its foundations on such principles, and organizing its powers in such form, as to them shall seem most likely to effect their safety and happiness."

This doctrine is true to reason and Scripture. It regards man not as the victim and slave of civil law, but as its proprietor and conservator, for the noblest objects of life. It regards government as made for man, and not man for government. The opposite view presents man as doomed to servitude, for the support of mere power. He is a drudge, on whose obsequiousness government officials may fatten, and who can only properly fulfill his obligations by submission in all things. That is, he is a being made to be governed, and made for nothing else. Hence, it is of no consequence whether he is well or ill governed, since government of any kind is presumed to meet all the demands of his nature.

Despots have assiduously inculcated this abominable error, because they well understood that truth would destroy their pretensions and annihilate their power. Every attempt has been made to surround the subject of government reform with superstitious fears, as though it were something too high or too sacred for the people to manage. Submission to the powers that be, without any exception, is the burden of political teaching. The people are made to believe that it is dangerous for them to meditate improvements and alterations in matters so vastly important, and so much above them! Just as though it was not altogether the people's business to attend to these things. Who shall look after the rights of the people—themselves, or those whom they have directed, as their servants, to discharge certain specified duties? Is it the duty of the people to look after their own interests, or is it not? Is it, in short, a crime in them to attend to their own affairs? Base is that sophistry, which would mislead the public on so vital a point. Statesmen, politicians, government officials, legislators, and all who live by the present order of things, in such a way as to dread salutary changes in civil polity, are conspirators against mankind. They delude the people, in order to destroy them.

"Their interest, like a lion, lives on prey."

From all such treasonable sentiments and designs, we cannot too earnestly pray to be delivered. The generations of men have too long groaned under the infamous deception practiced by civil despots. It is time the spell was broken. Men should know that "resistance to tyrants is obedience to God." It is not meddling—it is not impertinence for the people to assume the correction of political evils. The work is theirs, and only theirs, because, under God, they are the only fountain of civil authority. To array against them their own institution, is merciless barbarity: to make them destroy one another, for the ostensible purpose of promoting their welfare, is worse than savage cruelty. It has been said, that "the world is governed too much," and if the unprincipled usurpation to which we have just referred, must be set down as government, we shall have no difficulty in admitting the saying to be true. Of good government, there cannot be too much; like health, it can never accumulate to excess. But of miserable perversions, under the name of government, the world has had enough; and it is the unquestionable duty of all good men to use their best exertions to put down tyranny, wherever it may exist, either in church or state. This is the effect, and that directly, as well as indirectly, of the Gospel. The preaching of the pure word of God, is necessarily subversive of every form of human wickedness. This word binds men to the higher law, whatever may be the consequences, and whoever may command to the contrary. Patriotism does the same. It is quite as patriotic to break laws as to keep them, provided they are not what they should be. We may go even further, and affirm that patriotism absolutely demands resistance to bad laws. Such is the view taken of this important question, by Dr. Paley—an author who never leans to the side of ultraism:

> "It may be as much a duty, at one time, to resist government, as it is, at another, to obey it: to wit, whenever more advantage will, in our opinion, accrue from resistance, than mischief."—*Philos.: book* 6, *ch.* 3.

We have little disposition to enter upon refinements, on a subject of this magnitude, and hence, shall not waste time in discussing the difference between passive and active disobedience to law. It has been contended, that passive obedience is allowable, where active is not. But this is a distinction of no consequence, either practically or morally, for he who refuses to obey, is just as liable to punishment, as he who seeks to overturn the authority which imposed the unrighteous requirement.

CHAPTER VIII.

SLAVERY.

An application of the foregoing principles to slavery, necessarily involves an inquiry into the nature and effects of that institution. Is slavery accordant with the Higher Law, or is it not? This is the question, and the only question to be settled. If revelation and nature favor the institution, all attempts to put it down are wicked and must be abortive. The laws which sustain slavery, are either conformable to the higher law, or they are not: if the former is true, they should be cherished; if the latter, they should be abolished. As we most confidently believe the latter, and not the former, to be the fact in the case, we shall proceed to examine the character of slavery in three aspects—natural, political, and religious. In all these respects, it stands forth as the rankest INJUSTICE.

SECTION I.

NATURAL INJUSTICE OF SLAVERY.

The slave is a man, and, therefore, has the rights of a man. While he retains his humanity, he must retain all the rights belonging to humanity. At all events, these rights inhere in his nature, and are as inalienable as are the rights of any other human being. Whence, then, this abnegation of right—this total destruction of every privilege guarantied by the charter of existence? Plainly, from that depravity, which, ever since the Fall, has waged war against God, and against his creatures. But to ascertain the cause of this injustice, and to gauge its extent, are things very different; we may know that wrong has been done, and yet remain comparatively unmoved, because we are ignorant of the extent of the wrong. It is thus that slavery has too frequently passed without censure, as a venial fault; or provoked only a slight displacency, when it ought to have filled the soul with righteous indignation. Barely to affirm that the slave is divested of his natural rights, is not enough. We must enumerate those rights, and study their importance to the man himself, to the world in which he lives, and to the God who made him, or we cannot feel all the abhorrence towards the system of slavery, which its extreme wickedness deserves.

It is nevertheless true, that no possible care, or skill, on our part, can fully exhibit the injustice of this horrible institution. God alone can measure all the depths of its depravity. The following particulars embrace as full a statement as our limits will permit.

1. *Slavery takes away the right to life.* This first natural right of man, is not always openly repealed on the statute-books of slave-holding states and nations, but it is virtually repealed. The slave has no equal chance for self-defence. His master goes armed, but he is unarmed. And in case of resistance, the law always gives the master the right to kill his slave at once. If charged with crime, the law, not recognizing him as a man, withholds from him the protection which it affords to other criminals. We do not say that the slave may be killed wantonly, for such atrocity is not allowed, even towards brutes, but we affirm that his life is scarcely more secure than that of a brute. Whenever the master wishes to kill him, he can easily find what, in the eye of the law, will be a justifiable pretext.

2. *It takes away all personal liberty.* Beyond the exercise of those animal functions, indispensable to existence, the slave has neither liberty, nor the hope of liberty. Even those physical powers most necessary to his existence, are subjected to severe restrictions. He may not see, or hear, or speak, or eat, except as the master prescribes. Such

food and clothing as are given him, he may use, and no other; such words as his owner chooses, he may hear, and no other. The right to go where and when he will, and the right to do, or not to do, are not his. He must obey another in all things, or suffer whatever penalty his master chooses to inflict—it may be starving, scourging, maiming, selling, imprisonment, or death—for the law leaves him, as it does any other property, almost entirely at the owner's disposal.

3. *It destroys all self-ownership.* Every man has a natural right to himself—his own body and mind, with their various faculties and powers. Nothing of this kind can belong to the slave, because the law which makes him a slave strips him of the last vestige of self-control. His mind and body, with all their capabilities, are the property of another. He can own nothing, for the simple reason that he is nothing—a mere nullity in law, and as incapable of ownership as a horse or a tree. What protection the law gives to his life, is given, not because he has any rights, but merely to preserve him as property. The law does not allow of a wanton destruction of property, and hence some little regard is paid to the treatment of human, as well as other animals. Were there no other outrage on the rights of the slave, this alone is sufficient to strike him from the list of men. Without the right of possession, he must drift along the stream of life, blighted and paralyzed beyond re-

lief. The slave cannot be a man—the law will not allow it. The law, having made him a chattel personal, disdains to know him in any other capacity. And if he has more sensibility or power than a brute, it is only because he could not be dispossessed of these without destroying his life, and therefore his value as a chattel. The law has done its worst—it has taken all that could be taken, and is only restrained by the utter impossibility of inflicting further injury.

4. *It takes away conscience.* In subjecting the slave to the will of his master, conscience is entirely set aside. No man can have a conscience unless he has either the power of choice, as to what he shall do, or an assurance that whatever is required is infallibly correct. No slave can do right, except upon the mere contingency, that his owner will allow him to do so. That many who own slaves would consent to a course of rectitude, is not more certain than that there are many others who would not. Hence virtue is not provided for, and ought not to be expected to exist, in a slave population. It is not contemplated by the law, and too often not tolerated by the owner.

5. *It destroys the marriage relation.* So far as we have any knowledge, slaves are incapable of contracting marriage. They are, in this respect, exactly on a level with brutes. Indeed, it is not possible that marriage should exist, for marriage is a legal relation, and implies contracting power; but

the slave can make no contract. He is unknown in law, except as belonging exclusively and entirely to another. He may live as if married, but it would be a desecration of law to repeat its forms over those who have not power to keep the slightest of its requirements. The slave, if he could be married, could not protect his wife from insult and defilement, for she would not belong to him, but to his owner—all that the slave has, being his master's. Moreover, she might be sold or separated from him at any moment.

6. *It destroys the parental relation.* This follows inevitably from the foregoing. When marriage is not allowed to exist, the duty of parents to instruct and provide for their children must cease. Amid universal concubinage, parentage can scarcely be traced beyond the mother, and if it could, both mother and father are equally unable to provide for their children or themselves. But the chief difficulty is the want of authority. The slave is divested of all right to govern his children; they must obey their master, and not their parents. Again, the relation is destroyed, because the children of slaves may at any time be separated from their parents forever. Without means to support his children, without the right to govern them, or even to retain them within his knowledge, the slave has no power to discharge the duties of a parent.

7. *It takes away the right of self-improvement.* One of the most valuable of man's natural rights,

is that of developing his own powers. His physical, mental, and moral faculties require cultivation; but all education is denied him. Not only are no institutions of learning provided for his use, but the laws of every slave state make it a high misdemeanor to teach a slave to read. The slave is kept in brutal ignorance, that he may be kept a slave. His owner knows that knowledge and slavery are incompatible. All the cultivation allowed to his physical and moral powers, is of that questionable kind, which will fit him the better for a state of servitude. He may be taught submission and fidelity to his master, and so much of manual dexterity as will enable him to work in the field, like the horse or the ox. Other cultivation he cannot have, unless by stealth, and at the peril of greater hardships.

8. *It destroys the pursuit of happiness.* By cutting off all the rights which belong to man as man, it cuts off all the motives that prompt human nature to better its condition. The slave may toil, but the rewards of his toil are for another. He can neither have any thing, nor be any thing, but a chattel. His earnings are not at his disposal, so that if prompted by the most devoted affection to labor, he must labor in vain. Virtue and cultivation bring him nothing, except a keener sense of torment. His state of vassalage precludes all hope. He can never rise to manhood. And his posterity after him, to the latest hour of time,

shall lie just as low, and just as hopeless, as himself. For the slave there is nothing but brutal drudgery up to the day of death, and there would be nothing beyond, if human legislation could reach the "better land."

SECTION II.

POLITICAL INJUSTICE OF SLAVERY.

Slavery is the creature of law. It originates in the law, and depends upon it for its existence. Not that the law is more than a proximate cause, for the law itself must have a cause, and that cause, however remote, is the real basis of slavery, and of all slavery laws. This primary source of the evil, is, as we have already stated, the corruption of man's nature, which renders him not only unjust towards God, but also towards the creatures of God. But we have now to do only with the practical embodiment of this depravity, in the shape of political regulations. It is quite obvious, that men are naturally on a level, in relation to essential rights. Among the truths held to be self-evident, by the ever memorable signers of the Declaration of Independence—a class of men and a document, to which we cannot too often refer—this was first, and in these words, "all men are created equal." This was but re-affirming a great truth, which these patriots deemed too obvious for argumentation—it was simply throwing into words, one of the first dictates of common sense and common justice. It was no fortunate discovery or recondite speculation of theirs; they did no more than appeal to it as a truth, pre-established and indisputably evident to all men. Taking this, then, as our starting point, we must claim for the slave an equal chance in the advantages of civil government. If the institution is beneficial to others, it certainly must be beneficial to him, unless through his own fault, or that of others. But what is the actual result? This, and only this: slavery, at one fell swoop, strips its subjects of every political right. It is not a bare curtailment of civil immunities, but the entire loss of all—as if humanity itself were swept away. The slave becomes a chattel, and ceases to be a man. Still further, to illustrate this fact, I shall specify some of the more prominent features of the slave code.

1. *The slave has no part in making the laws.* To all others, except under the most absolute monarchies, where laws can hardly be said to exist, some chance is afforded of determining what the law shall be. If all do not sit in legislative assemblies, or even have the right of suffrage, they are, nevertheless, represented, because the laws are made for men; and their humanity is represented in the humanity of those who do make the laws. Legislators legislate for themselves, as well as for others,

and they make such laws for other freemen or citizens, as they themselves expect to keep. But the citizenship of the slave is denied. He comes not into the category of men; he is not regarded as human. The laws which bear upon him, bear upon no one else; they are slave laws—made to degrade men, and keep them degraded. And so far as the slave is concerned, none of the ordinary ends of government are had in view, in these enactments. His protection and improvement, his welfare and happiness, are wholly out of the question. The legislation concerns the master, not the slave.

2. *The slave has no part in administering the laws.* Of course, this is only in keeping with the preceding. It might, however, be some alleviation, if such inhuman laws could be impartially administered. But severe and ruinous as is the law, its actual administration is, after all, more shocking. Caprice, ignorance, lust, avarice, pride, madness, tyranny, all by turns or at once, stimulate to abuse, and where the law itself is so exceeding brutal, it must, of necessity, under the influence of these depraved passions, become a convenient instrument of unmeasured wrongs. The slave has no redress. Submission or death are the only alternatives. It is conceded, that all slave-holders may not be thus severe, but the ground of complaint is, that all *may be* what the worst indisputably are. There can be no security, so long as the law cuts off the slave from all participation in guarding his own rights.

3. *The slave is treated as a culprit, and that without any alleged guilt.* One would naturally suppose that a criminal would at least have some of the usual forms of justice applied to him. But we see nothing in his case, except the most perfect disinheritance. As if predestinated to utter ruin—as if all the possibilities of manhood had been forfeited forever—he is unscrupulously allotted to servitude, with only such legislative oversight as will keep him in implicit subjection to his owner. There is no imputation of personal guilt, and the infliction can have respect to nothing but ancestral or imaginary demerit. Neither of these, however, is alleged, and the worse than felon's condition, imposed upon the African, must be acknowledged to be without any assignable cause. He is a slave, and, therefore, must be a slave—this is the only reason given for the contumely and outrage heaped upon his nature. Whether this is a sufficient reason, I shall not now inquire.

4. *The slave law takes away all property, and all the rights of property.* No slave can sue or be sued, because he cannot be the owner of any thing—not even of himself. This is the most perfect alienation possible. It reduces the individual to a nonentity. How disastrous such a state must be, will readily be perceived, when we reflect that by far the larger part of human laws relate, either directly or indirectly, to property interests. It diminishes the slave code to the merest fragment, making it con-

sist of a few precepts and penalties—but chiefly the latter—for the regulation of personal conduct. All the great interests of humanity perish at once, under this heartless system, and the slave becomes as isolated from the rest of the human race, as if God had made him only what his owner makes him—a brute. Such a living death is the inevitable lot of all, to whom the law is nothing but a record of penalties. It is the object of government to conserve all the rights of man; in this case, however, it does exactly the reverse, and destroys them all. But there is here no inconsistency with the avowed principle of the slave code, for it everywhere assumes that the slave is not a man.

5. The next particular, is a *total restriction of personal liberty.* No more is allowed the slave, in this respect, than is allowed the cattle of the field. He may go where his owner permits, but no where else. But the condition of the slave falls much below that of the brute; since the latter may stray with impunity, while the former is liable to the severest punishment, for such an offence. Both are considered as personal property, and neither may leave his owner without permission. Such a law cuts off all emigration, and nearly all business of a commercial nature, except in the slave states. It renders those changes and removals, which are prompted by industry and enterprise, an utter impossibility. And if there were no other unjust laws bearing upon the slave, this alone would ensure his

ruin. Give him all the other rights of manhood, but take away personal freedom, and all his energies will remain dormant.

6. *The slave is subjected to disproportioned punishments.* The penal code of slavery is not only made and administered, irrespective of the right which every man has to regulate the civil institute under which he lives, but it bears the stamp of intentional cruelty. Degradation is its object. The slave is to be made to feel that he is not human, and, therefore his faults are punished with a severity unknown to human jurisprudence. In the first place, the law imposes upon him a great many restrictions, such as could be imposed only by the most intolerable tyranny, and then seeks to enforce the observance of these restrictions by bloody penalties. These shocking, demoniacal barbarities, are worthy of that supreme wickedness, for the support of which they are employed.

7. *The laws afford him no protection.* It has been shown, in the previous section, that even life is not guarded by the slave law. All other rights are swept away at once, by converting him into a chattel, and if life were not essential to the value of the chattel, there is every reason to believe the slave would be killed with as little ceremony as any other animal. As the law now stands, he is exposed to the fury of the most diabolical passions, and may be mutilated or slaughtered, whenever his master chooses, provided some decent excuse can be in-

vented, to cover the deed of infamy. All other indignities follow, of course. Where life is not protected, it is in vain to look for the protection of other rights. Thus, the very object for which law exists among men, is wholly lost sight of, and the slave is as completely shut out from every advantage of this kind, as if he had not been created a member of the human family.

8. *The laws afford him no assistance whatever.* Instead of the kindly aid, which government was designed to give to every human being, the slave experiences nothing but systematic spoliation. Government, though a blessing to others, is to him the severest curse. He reaps none of the good which it might do, but suffers all the evils which its utmost perversion can inflict. An institution that others regard as the charter of rights, is, to him, only a record of perpetual disinheritance. Not one of all the numerous advantages of association can he know, inasmuch as the law has cast him beyond its pale, and heeds him only as a being made to be spoiled.

SECTION III.

RELIGIOUS INJUSTICE OF SLAVERY.

Slavery and Christianity are eternal opposites, as separate from each other as vice is from virtue, or heaven from hell. This is a truth, almost too well

known to need illustration, but we will briefly state the facts on which the declaration is made, and which forever place slavery in the category of crimes.

1. *It is opposed to the law of love.* Christianity teaches us to love God with all the heart, and our neighbor as ourselves. Neither can be done by him who robs a fellow being of liberty, and of every other essential right. It is no worse to rob a man of money, than it is to rob him of that which is equivalent to money. The crime of robbing does not consist in taking money or goods simply, but in taking that which is valuable; it is forcibly invading another's rights. Now, if liberty is of any value to the colored man, the law of love will not allow him to be dispossessed of it, unless for reasons of a punitive nature, and no one pretends that slavery is designed as a punishment. Love requires that we should be quite as willing to become a slave, as to impose that condition on another. It avails nothing to say, that others have imposed the condition, and that we have only acquiesced in what was already done; for we may as well kill the prophets as build their tombs, if, by our conduct, we sanction their murder. To keep stolen property, when it is known to have been stolen, and when it is in our power to return it to the owner, is the basest injustice—is theft. Men are brethren, and one great object of the gospel is, to restore fraternal feeling to the human heart; but this cannot be done

without annihilating slavery, which is at war with all fraternal feelings.

2. *It is opposed to the law of improvement.* Christianity improves all who come under its influence; it is an elevating power, which never fails to raise both the head and the heart to higher excellence. But slavery crushes the whole man, and keeps him forever crushed—a thing of naught, neither man nor brute. Such a being cannot be a Christian, nor can Christianity produce such a forlorn thing—a being so blighted, wrecked, hopeless. It may seem a bold proposition, but we affirm, that whether we contemplate the master or the slave, Christianity is impossible to the relation. Could the slave remain as ignorant and powerless as he was before his conversion, then he might still be a slave, but by virtue of his translation into the kingdom of Christ, he is made free: 1. From every law of man which conflicts with his obligation to God. 2. From that imbecility peculiar to ignorance. 3. From irresponsibility, or that absence of all character, which makes the mere chattel. The slave, as a heathen, has no rights, no conscience, no wife, no children. But Christianity strips him quickly of this irresponsibility, and restores his manhood, by giving him duties to perform, with which no other man may interfere. The converted slave is, therefore, by the very fact of his conversion, brought under an authority which destroys all human ownership in him, and all improper control over him. The

master is restrained in like manner. He may not keep a slave, because he cannot keep, innocently, a human being degraded; he is bound to labor for the intellectual, moral, and physical improvement of all mankind. Show us any class of men, towards whom the Christian may even be indifferent, and then we will admit that religion does not necessarily destroy the relation of slave and master.

3. *It is opposed to the law of purity.* Holiness, or moral purity, is one of the most essential principles of the gospel, but slavery is a violation of right, and therefore, cannot be consistent with a system that forbids all wrong—all unholiness. Few men have ever been so fool-hardy, as to attempt to prove that slavery is right, *per se.* Such an attempt could only show that the man who made it, had no proper ideas of right and wrong—that, in his mind, vice and virture were all the same, or were distinguished from each other by something which had no relation to human happiness. Is it right to hold a man as a slave? Certainly not. The common sense, the feelings, and the judgment of men, are as much united in denying the justice of slavery, as they are in denying that of murder. Now, as a holy religion cannot sanction an unholy practice, it follows, invariably, that wherever the gospel prevails, slavery must cease. All Christians, and all Christian ministers, will behold it with abhorrence, and enquire, "What shall be done for the extirpation of the evil of slavery?"

4. *It is opposed to the law of equality.* The gospel is a system of spiritual agrarianism. It puts the prince and the peasant on a level, giving to each in proportion to his faith, and only in proportion to his faith. In the church there is neither high nor low, neither great nor small. Slavery disturbs this equality, and instead of putting all on a level, where the God of nature and of grace puts them, it gives to one man all power, and to the other none. This is unchristian, because it is unkind. It is not doing to the colored man, as the white man wishes should be done to himself. It is unbrotherly, cruel, unjust. And in fact, the whole question of emancipation, whether immediate or gradual, is simply a question of justice. Slavery is injustice—unprovoked, inexcusable, and immeasurable injustice. The colored man has just the same right—if right there can be—to subject the white man to bondage, to hold him, with his wife and his children, as chattels, subject to separation and to sale. The white man need not be shocked at this, for when we come to the abstract justice of slavery, the color of the skin makes no difference. Eternal justice demands that the slave go free. His bondage is a fraud on creation. Those who hold him, and those who consent to his being held as a slave, are the guilty perpetrators of this fraud. It is not for us to say how far they *mean* to be fraudulent, and to pervert the justice of the All-creating Hand which dispenses the gift of freedom to each

alike; we are witnesses to the fact only, and have no power to determine the exact turpitude of the motives which influence the oppressor. His proud wrath may be less criminal than we had supposed, but the natural history of slavery reveals itself everywhere as a violence done to nature. Hence, though for political reasons we might wish to avoid extremes, yet moral rectitude allows of no compromise. There is no middle ground. We must either let the oppressed go free, or ourselves be worse than slaves—unjust. Had men no consciences, they might innocently be slave-holders, but as the case now stands, the white man must become a knave if the colored man becomes a slave. The struggle, therefore, is to avoid guilt. The North may be moved partly by sympathy, but by far the sternest motive known to anti-slavery men is, a sense of that equal justice which is ever due from man to man.

5. *It is opposed to the law of truth.* Religion is true; it is founded in truth, and inculcates only truth. But slavery is false, fundamentally false, and leads all astray who have any thing to do with it. The master, the slave, civilization, and religion, are alike ruined by its influence. Christianity never leaves a man with so little light, as to make him the victim of such an error. He who thinks to prosper by oppression, mistakes the economy of Providence. The poor and the ignorant are to be raised up, and made equal with other men; this is the way to prosperity, as indicated by the gospel,

and it is no wonder that the slave states, acting for generations in open disregard of so important a truth, should steadily decline, while all around them is flourishing in the highest degree. It is but the blight and curse which always follow sin.

6. *It is opposed to the law of God as God.* Not, indeed, if we concede that slavery is in accordance with the Divine law, for then the master becomes as God—his tyranny is but an expression of the Divine will. And this sort of justification, it is well known, is a prime object with all slavery propagandists. They affect to be executing the predetermined purpose of Heaven; and when this subterfuge will not answer, they claim that God has delegated all power to civil government, and that the decrees of such government cannot be resisted without sin. This hypothesis, it is true, does not affect slavery alone: it crushes at once all religious freedom, and makes men obey the state, whether it bids them do right or wrong. When there is a plain conflict between the Divine and human, the latter must always have precedence. It is clear, therefore, that the kingdom of God cannot be established in connection with such pretensions, unless it takes the form of politics, and identifies itself always with the dominant party. But such fatalism, or pantheism, is the merest evasion of all argument, and in practice amounts to downright atheism. The substance is this: slavery must be sanctioned at all events, and neither God nor man may teach or prac-

tice to the contrary. We therefore conclude, that the law of God cannot be known among slave-holders as the law of God, because in this character it might have inconvenient claims—it would be superior to any law they could make, and this superiority would reduce their slavery code to a nullity.

These general considerations are amply sufficient to show that the spirit of Christianity is subversive of slavery, and that there is no safety for the peculiar institution but in the absence of religion. Where the gospel is, slavery cannot be. They can never coalesce. It is, however, not the spirit alone of the gospel that is opposed to slavery; the letter is equally hostile to every thing of the kind. We admit that slavery is not specifically prohibited in the New Testament. Neither are murder, burglary, counterfeiting, and various other high crimes. Shall we conclude that these are consistent with Christianity, because they are not particularly specified among its prohibitions? We are enjoined to do no evil, to be holy, and to be kind, and these general precepts are a literal prohibition of slavery, with all its kindred abominations.

How far religion may exist in connection with the bare form of slavery, aside from its spirit, I do not pretend to determine. But as the slave law is unjust, Christianity must of necessity render it a dead letter; the two cannot co-exist. It may be possible, that in some rare instances the spirit of the institution is so entirely dead, that though the form remains, it is innocuous. Still, the presence of such an instrument of tyranny, is always good evidence that the spirit of tyranny is also present. The laws of a people are a true index to their dispositions. Were only the dead letter of the law remaining, as is often alleged in favor of those who hold slaves, it would nevertheless be very dangerous to continue in such a relation. These dead laws would be a temptation to cruelty and injustice; the evil spirit would come again to inhabit those souls from which it had been expelled, and to revive the laws which had become dead. Safety requires that the letter, as well as the spirit of the law, should be extirpated, for the one begets the other. But this is mainly a question of prudence, and I shall not detain the reader with a further discussion of it.

CHAPTER IX.

THE EFFECTS OF SLAVERY.

Simple injustice, however enormous, is by no means expressive of all the evils that belong to slavery. To the deliberate crushing of a race, there must be added that long list of sad effects which so surely follows, whenever the rights of humanity are trampled down. These evil consequences are inseparable from the system, and may be distinctly seen in every slave-holding community. They relate to the slave, the slave-holder, and the state.

SECTION I.

EFFECTS ON THE SLAVE.

The birds-eye view which we took of slavery, in the preceding chapter, though far from exhibiting all its colossal wickedness, was sufficient to demonstrate that the slave must sink to the deepest wretchedness. His rights gone, and all the incentives to improvement taken away, his very humanity crushed, and every hope of regaining it lost, it would be folly to expect any thing but the most perfect degradation. As he has no opportunities above a brute, he will, of course, become brutal. He can aspire to nothing higher than the gratification of his animal appetites, because there is nothing higher within his reach—nothing else allowed him by the law, and not even this, except under severe restrictions. Slaves are proverbially inefficient laborers, but this is only a natural result of compelling them to work in the absence of proper motives. What they earn is not theirs; and white men would be just as dilatory and worthless, if obliged to toil under the same circumstances. They are also comparatively useless, owing to the extreme ignorance in which they must be kept. The mechanic arts and the sciences cannot be taught them, without disqualifying them for servitude. In fact, the very knowledge which would fit them for any branch of business, would melt their chains. It is therefore necessary to keep them ignorant in order to keep them at all. Knowledge is power, and slaves are allowed no power, lest they should use it for their own good. Everywhere, then, this kind of population must exhibit the imbecility of ignorance.

Poverty follows in the train of compulsory ignorance. The slave has nothing. He is kept so degraded that but little could be his, if he were permitted to have what he earns. His ignorant drudgery would only yield a scanty support at best; yet even this is not afforded him, and he is forced to subsist, not as a man, but as an animal. And he is clothed and housed as he is fed; that is, in the coarsest manner, and on such a scanty allowance as may be convenient, after the owner's cupidity and luxury have been provided for, out of this unpaid and unproductive labor.

The next effect of the system is its total perversion of the nobler instincts of the soul. It strikes out of man's nature all that is human, and leaves a wreck. It dwarfs into a brute, a being which God intended for a man. This is the sin of slavery. This is its grand effect. The beings thus despoiled are not dead, but ruined; their physical nature is not dead, but their humanity is. Neither the cares, nor the aspirations, nor the hopes, nor the duties, nor the motives, which ought to actuate man, are ever known to these degraded beings. The beneficence and wisdom of the Creator are set at naught. He might as well have made the African incapable of the functions of humanity, since the slave-holder decides that these functions shall never be exercised. So much is done in the first generation towards dehumanizing the slave; and if the effects of the system are so disastrous on the first generation, what must they be when accumulated in his nature by means of hereditary transmission? It is precisely this superinduced weakness and meanness which give to slavery its permanence, and to the master his security. He has succeeded in growing a race of men—men only in form—fitted for servility.

As the slave cannot be trusted with knowledge, so neither can he be trusted with any of the results of knowledge. Machinery, now of such transcendent importance to all civilized countries, is a thing next to impossible where slavery exists. To work machinery requires intelligence; but the utmost pains are taken—even to the enactment of severe prohibitory laws—to keep the slave in ignorance. He is therefore doomed to incapability, and must forego all the advantages which mechanical invention has conferred upon the world. That is, he must be a savage; for it amounts to this, since there is little difference between civilized and uncivilized, except in the state of the arts and sciences.

SECTION II.

EFFECTS ON THE SLAVE-HOLDER.

By a law of Providence, the injurer as well as the injured, suffers. The doer of wrong cannot escape the effects of his own conduct. That law which forces the slave to lose caste among human beings, is scarcely less ruinous to his master. The industry, that should have promoted health and virtue, is dispensed with, and all the deplorable consequences of idleness follow. Labor is deemed fit only for slaves, and hence the master, together with his children, falls into habits of sloth and effeminacy, as discreditable as they are pernicious. Such habits are not only evil in themselves, and in their effects upon the slave-owner, but they subtract from the common store, by just so much as the well-directed industry of those who are idle would have earned. And this is another source of the poverty common to all slave-holding states. Wealth is the fruit of toil. But where only a part, say one-half, labor, and these under the greatest disadvantage, because of the profound ignorance in which they must be kept, extreme poverty is an unavoidable consequence. In estimating the wealth of slave-holding communities, we are liable to miscalculate, inasmuch as the entire body of slaves have nothing, and are expected to have nothing. If the few slave-owners are not degradingly poor, it is because they are the only property-holders. It will be found, moreover, that their wealth is often wholly fictitious, consisting of what, in other states, is never called property—namely, the bodies and souls of men. This is not wealth, and would not be regarded as such, in a free country: yet it makes by far the larger part of all the riches of a slave-holding people. How degraded and impoverished must be that community, which has to inventory the bones and sinews of one half of its number as property, in order that the other half may be said to have wealth! The expedient fails, however, and with all their sacrilegious counting of men as property, the slave states are, and must be, wretchedly poor.

Their poverty, notwithstanding it is extreme, is only a minor evil. Released from the salutary toil which enriches freemen, slave-holders sink into dissipation and debauchery. An idle people must ever be vicious as well as poor. But their vices flow chiefly from another source; having broken down all law and all right, on the part of their slaves, this absence of restraint becomes a copious fountain of corruption. Indeed, the first act in this drama of crime draws after it all the rest. The slave is plundered in the outset of every thing pertaining to him as a man, and this commencement indicates the spirit which is to control his subsequent history. One crime naturally follows another, and those who have left their victim defenceless, will be sure to yield to the temptation which such a state offers to the commission of further crimes. Strike down the right of a man to protect himself from insult, and he is sure to be treated as a brute; take from woman the right to defend her virtue, and she is equally sure to become polluted. Whether this utter corruption was intended or not, by those who first instituted slavery, is of little moment, since the fact of its existence cannot be questioned. That the most shocking cruelty, and the grossest licentiousness abound, wherever slavery is tolerated, is too apparent to need proof—is admitted even by slave-holders themselves. Nor is this corruption optional with either the slaves or their masters. The relation of the parties being unnatural and criminal in itself, leads inevitably to further wickedness. The spirit which degraded the man or woman, is necessary to keep such man or woman degraded. The same crushing, robbing, polluting, heartless invasion of rights, must be kept up to the last. Under a better spirit, slavery would soon become extinct, and that, too, without legislative aid. Its enormities could not be perpetrated by pure minds. The system being the opposite of virtue, would be a flat impossibility among the virtuous. A good *regime* can never know such a monstrosity. The dreadful necessity, then, is imposed on every slave-holder, of personally and intentionally enslaving man. He cannot be a mere inheritor of slaves, but in order to hold them, must acquire the same dispositions which originally reduced them to bondage. This is not theory, but fact. The child of every slave mother is as really made a slave, by the owner of the mother, as if it had been purchased in Africa for the purpose of enslavement. And in this way slave-holders are not barely holding the slaves which past generations had entailed upon them, but actually enslaving all the children who are born of slave parents. Hence, whatever guilt may be affirmed of the first slave-holder, may be affirmed of all his successors. No child is born a slave, or can be; such a thing is unknown in nature. But as the children of slaves are all made slaves, it follows that slave-holders, notwithstanding their pretensions to chivalry, are guilty of preying upon helpless infancy, and robbing it of every right—even its very humanity. Infancy, which always finds protection among the good, is thus cruelly outraged by slave-holders. This dastardly, ignoble conduct has no parallel in human wickedness. Compared with it, ordinary robbery appears but a venial fault. It has none of the courage which marks the brigand. It has no redeeming qualities; it is sheer depravity, deliberately blotting out all the traces of manhood, and cutting off all the possibilities of happiness. But I will not dwell on this reproachful aspect of the subject.

Aside from the evils just enumerated, is another, less observed, but scarcely less pernicious. I allude to the wanton contempt for MAN, which this abominable system renders necessary. Not only towards the slave is there unfeeling and unbrotherly treatment, but a habit of tyrannizing is formed, which displays itself in implacable resentment and murderous strife, whenever opportunity offers. The sanctity of man is destroyed. Hands, that have so often stripped human nature of its all, save life, and that without any provocation whatever, can hardly be expected to deal kindly and respectfully with more than a few personal and partisan friends. It is just this want of regard for man as man, that has made all attempts to abolish slavery so difficult. A peculiar recklessness of life and character, a fierce and almost insane devotion to existing usages, irrespective of right or wrong, have rendered every effort at improvement, both dangerous and impracticable. We cannot account for this, except on the ground of moral deterioration. Slave-holders seem to have no interest in human progress—certainly none, but directly the reverse, in reference to their slaves; and the necessity which they are under to maintain this hostility to the improvement of some, naturally makes them indifferent, if not hostile, to the improvement of all. This inertia, or misanthropy of character, is the clue to the utter despair which prevails in all slave-holding states, touching the success of emancipation. The public mind, in such communities, is so unused to enterprize, that it halts, with childish dread, at difficulties which would only provoke a more determined trial among the pure and the vigorous. As purity is power, and impurity is weakness, none have a vigorous moral purpose, but those in whom conscience has its full sway. Hence, there is moral atrophy wherever there is slavery.

Again, slavery does not afford opportunity for cultivating the higher virtues. It is necessary to refrain from great plans of improvement, lest the slave interest be subverted thereby. No schemes of amelioration, no means of elevation, are wanted, in such a community. It would jeopard the "peculiar institution," to cherish such designs in its presence. We accordingly find either an utter stagnation of thought in such communities, on all the subjects of practical benevolence, or, what is much the same, these thoughts are confined to the relief of those in remote countries—the heathen of other lands, instead of their own.

I do not affirm that all who have to do with slavery are equally affected by the system. Its disastrous consequences may be less fatal to some than to others; but the tendency of the system is always the same, and all who come under its influence, must be depraved, more or less. So true is this, that it is doubtful which suffers most from slavery—the slave or his master.

SECTION III.

ITS EFFECTS ON THE STATE.

As might be expected, every slave country has its uncontrollable evils. These defy all exact enumeration, and all precise measurement; but we may profit by a hasty glance at them. First, then, we notice the absence of cultivation. In order to tillage and husbandry—such as belong to agricultural thrift—it is necessary that at least the heavier restraints of industry be thrown off. The ignorance, the want of motive, and the want of implements, which characterize slave labor, are insurmountable obstacles to the culture of the soil. Men, as chattels or animals, have sinews, and may perform various operations on land, but they will never cultivate it with success. They lack the means for such a work. No country was ever thoroughly improved, and its resources developed, by such laborers. Something may be done, and is done, or slavery could not exist; but the full capacity of the soil for production, is never elicited under such circumstances. In the Southern states, large portions of the country, once fertile, have actually deteriorated, until they have become worthless, and their occupants have had to seek new plantations. Such an occurrence was never known in a free country. But it is by no means uncommon, where slave-holding is practiced, or where, from extreme tyranny, all citizens are reduced to comparative vassalage. South America, Southern and Western Europe, Asia, Africa, and, in short, all countries having barbarous and tyrannical governments, furnish abundant proof of this. We look to them in vain for comfortable dwellings, beautiful fields, good roads, well supplied markets, for churches, schools, hospitals, and all the nameless productions of well directed industry.

Political insecurity is another, yet more striking feature, of slave-holding states. It is always unsafe to do wrong. And where one part of society is smarting under the lash, and goaded to desperation by the loss of all its civil rights, we may well anticipate, that the other part will feel diminished confidence in their own political safety. Quiet is incompatible with outrage. A consciousness of guilt—of the wrongs he has inflicted—makes the slave-holder more timid than other men. He fears the African, because he knows what reason there is for retaliation. "The wicked flee when no man pursueth; but the righteous are bold as a lion." It is not the ordinary depravity of human nature that slave-holders have to dread; they could guard against that, as other communities do. But they well know, that the usual safeguards of society are not enough for that superadded danger, which springs from oppression. This accounts for the fear of insurrection, so prevalent in all slave-holding states. People, wronged and degraded, are very likely to seek redress, and nothing but extreme ignorance, on the part of those who are thus treated, can prevent their instant self-emancipation. They might not retaliate upon their former masters, but they could not fail to throw off the fetters of slavery.

Every slave state is pervaded by this necessary inquietude and insecurity. And, as a consequence, we perceive everywhere a half military aspect. The police regulations, the customs and manners of society, and the tone of feeling, have a martial character. The arbitraments of such a people are not those of the civil courts; the lash, the pistol, and the bowie knife, more commonly decide their quarrels, and mete out what they term justice. Such brutal, uncivilized practices, are inseparable from slave masters, in their intercourse with each other, because they are forced to maintain this kind of conduct towards their slaves. Slavery knows no law but the law of force — brute force — and the master has, at all times, to evince his disposition and ability to compel the slave to be a slave. This necessity, everywhere existing in slave states, makes them exceedingly repulsive to freemen. It is like spending one's life in a military camp; it is as if civil liberty and peace were banished from the world.

There is yet another evil connected with all slave-holding countries. I allude to their inability to repel foreign invasion. It is true, that some opposition may be made to hostile forces, but the military strength of a slave state is greatly diminished, because slaves are not only not available, as soldiers, but require, for their safe keeping, the presence of others, who, apart from the danger of insurrection at home, might be employed as soldiers. Slave-holders must keep up a sort of standing army; the institution demands a continual guard, however unable the country may be to afford it.

Society may exist in such a country; there may be families and neighborhoods, hamlets, villages, and cities. These are not absolute impossibilities, and yet, from the very nature of the case, they must exist under many embarrassments, and in a much less perfect condition, than characterizes them in free states. In the first place, a large part of the citizens are socially dead—non-existent. This widens the distance between actual neighbors, and cuts off, in so far, all the advantages of association. In the city, a population of fifty thousand sinks to half that number—throwing upon these all the cares, and but half the advantages, common to a city twice as large. The same is true of villages, and rural districts. Schools, churches, and all things depending upon association, are poorly supported, because the existence of caste renders so many unavailable for social enterprizes. As a further illustration of this extreme weakness of slave-holding communities, we may notice the singular provision of our Federal Constitution. Slaves are not men—no, not even human beings—but in order that the slave states might not be wholly outnumbered in the popular branch of Congress, it was necessary to allow every five slaves to count as much as three free white men. This gives the South an advantage, which would not be necessary, if slavery had not so weakened that part of the Union as to render it incapable of standing upon equal terms with the free states. According to the views maintained by slave-holders, they might just as well have made their cattle and horses the basis of Congressional representation. But the free states saw the weakness of the slave-holding states, and yielded, on the principle that the strong ought to bear the burdens of the weak. The same disordered and enfeebled condition is discoverable at every point, in the history and circumstances of a slaveholding people.

I have thus briefly surveyed slavery, and its effects. The reader will need no suggestion as to what inferences he shall draw from such premises. If civil government was instituted for beneficent purposes, it certainly must be horribly perverted, before it can occasion the enormous abuses which we have just contemplated. On the governed and the governors, these evils fall with equal certainty, and almost equal severity. The one are robbed by force, the other, by committing the robbery, are doomed to still greater loss. Of the two, the slave is less injured than his master. That such an institution has any claims upon mankind, or that, for any cause, it ought to be exempted from the most rigorous opposition, is an idea too absurd to be entertained for a moment. An imaginary self-interest may blind the eyes of some, and the common hallucination, that slavery is a delicate and difficult affair to remove, may blind the eyes of others; but the essential turpitude and folly of the thing will always stamp it as an intolerable evil.

CHAPTER X.

SLAVERY A CRIME.

It is utterly impossible that such a system should be recognized as a Divine institution. It tramples upon every law of God, and defeats every benevolent purpose of his providence. The very term *slave*, implies a crime. Such a relation, of one human being to another human being, is itself evidence of guilt; it implies the subversion of rights, which God has made inalienable, and which no one but himself may innocently revoke or annul.

On this ground we rest. Here the anti-slavery cause finds its ample and eternal justification. Crime admits of no defence. The higher law not only allows, but compels every man to seek the destruction of vice. Does any one pretend to the contrary? Is it not a conceded fact, that both human and Divine laws require the extirpation of all wrong, or rather, abstinence from all wrong? There is no denial of this, except by resorting to downright atheism. But some allege that slavery is not, upon the whole, an evil, much less a crime; and this allegation is considered sufficient to silence both the accusations of conscience, and the reproofs of an indignant Christian public. Who is ignorant of such sophistry? Who has not witnessed it again and again, in every moral conflict? It is nothing more than a simple disturbance of established principles, in order to avoid the consequences which flow from them. It is a cheat of wicked men, to escape detection. The villain who keeps false weights, or false measures, acts on exactly the same plan. He appears to do right, only because the rule, by which right and wrong are determined, has been intentionally perverted—he gives full weight according to his scales, but not according to the scales of an honest man. Let the tyrant—the oppressor—the slave-holder—define justice, and slave-holding ceases to be unjust. It would be folly to dispute against the rectitude of slavery, if we acknowledged the authority of such ethics.

Slavery stands forth as a crime only when tried by an incorruptible rule. The law of God, in revelation and in nature, fixes its character beyond the possibility of mistake. There either is no wrong, or slavery is wrong—all wrong—most criminally and palpably wrong. Make expedience, or selfishness, or lust, or power, the test of rectitude, and slavery is at once established as a righteous practice; but not slavery alone, for pride, extravagance, theft, dueling, and murder, are sanctioned by the same authority. When we depart from the word of God, and from that instinctive sense of right which characterizes man as a rational being, there is no longer any restraint upon conduct. Moral distinctions cease, and custom, irrespective of right or wrong, becomes the only acknowledged standard of duty.

To such fearful lengths must they go, who either hold slaves or approve of slave-holding. It would be too much to avow respect for such an enormity. The evil must be disguised, or it cannot be endured. Even the most wicked, no less than novices in crime, demand something in the shape of justification—they must have an opiate to soothe the pangs of remorse, and prevent the entire loss of self-respect. In its naked character of sin, slavery finds little or no countenance; the shameless and abandoned atheist may possibly work himself up to such madness as would sanction it, *per se*, for he glories in his shame, and purposely reverses all natural sentiments of right. But to man, as he commonly meets us—to man, without any studied perversion of his judgment or instincts—to man, especially, enlightened by the word of God—slavery is unendurable, because it is slavery. The word is odious; it bespeaks outrage and wrong of no ordinary degree. There is an undefinable repugnance to every thing comprehended in the term. It is like the word *murder*—a word which expresses only horrible and revolting ideas—a word which has no associations that can please, or were ever designed to please. This word slavery has in it nothing that humanity can approve — nothing against which it does not instantly revolt; and there is, therefore, no way for one man to own another man as a slave. Manhood and slavery can never coalesce. The two are opposites, eternal and irreconcilable. And it is only by means of deception that they are ever made to have the appearance of harmonizing. Men adopt false notions of right, and then acquit themselves of all blame in robbing their fellow men of humanity. In this way deeds are done that would never be tolerated, if the true principles of morals were suffered to be applied to them. No man was ever the apologist of slavery, except as modified in the manner we have now suggested.

Though slavery is a crime, and must involve all concerned in it in guilt, we do not affirm that the form of slavery must always be accompanied by the spirit. The shadow may be where the substance is not. A bad law among a good people becomes a dead letter. Thus Washington and Jefferson — the most distinguished of patriots — were slave-holders only in name. Born amid slavery, and connected with it, not voluntarily but involuntarily, they contracted no fellowship or respect for the system, and did what they could for its subversion. There are, undoubtedly, thousands now connected with slavery who abhor the institution, and would gladly break away from its chains. Such are not to be classed with ordinary slave-holders, for with them slave-holding is merely a nominal thing, and if all were like them it would soon be abolished.

While we make this concession cheerfully, in view of special cases, it by no means follows that such an apology is generally applicable. The most who hold slaves, hold them intentionally and from choice. They approve of the system, and would gladly perpetuate it forever. With these, as with other culprits, reason and reproof are too apt to be useless; their heart is in the transgression, and to admonish them is to "cast pearls before swine." At first they may have had no relish for slave-holding, but as the practice of vice too commonly generates the love of vice, they are found at last warmly attached to what an upright and uncontaminated mind must always view with abhorrence. Slavery is contrary to the instincts of humanity—it contravenes the common sense, the obvious equality of natural rights, and the moral feelings which belong to the race. Nor can it ever be viewed as right, till the blindness induced by sin has dimned the sight and betrayed the judgment.

Slavery, considered as a crime, is necessarily abhorred. Human nature has never yet attained so desperate a stage of corruption as to hate unmixed good, or to love unmixed evil. We can call good evil, and hate it; or evil good, and love it; but we cannot hate the one and love the other, by itself alone. Hence, all approbation of slavery implies deception; the individual has voluntarily brought upon himself this blindness, or it has been caused involuntarily by the circumstances in which he has been placed; in either case, the immutability of constitutional principles is maintained, and virtue vindicated. It must be shown to be right to enslave men, or men — so God has made them — must abominate slavery.

CHAPTER XI.

APOLOGIES FOR SLAVERY.

As intimated in the foregoing chapter, slavery cannot stand alone—its essential wickedness makes it repulsive to all enlightened men. It is obvious that nothing but the unimportant circumstance of color, prevents the extension of the system to the utmost limit of power. And how long such a feeble barrier will be able to resist the encroachments of tyranny, must be very uncertain in any given case, since might, and not right, is the rule of progress. The possibility of a wider application of the slave-holding principle, is not simply a theoretical idea; it is already realized in Russia, in most Asiatic countries, and in Africa. The slavery of these countries has no relation to color, for the master and his slave are generally of the same complexion. In these nations, slavery itself constitutes a caste, without the trifling accident of color. This is also true of the slavery of the ancients. And if the disposition to enslave has, in other ages and nations, been exercised on those of kindred blood, we have reason to apprehend that the same may occur in our own country at some future time. Thus the institution comes home to every man's personal feelings, and menaces him with a doom as wretched as that now inflicted on the black man. The white man is secured only by the color of his skin, and how long that will protect him he cannot tell. He, therefore, sees himself in remote, if not in immediate danger, and the instinct of self-preservation renders him an enemy of slavery.

The honest fears, as well as moral repugnance, which cultivated men naturally entertain towards the system, have led its abettors to put forth a show of defence. But from first to last, not one argument has transpired, that does not make tenfold more against the system than for it. I shall not trouble the reader with a specific and formal refutation of all the various sophistries that have been employed in defence of the institution: it is enough that we select one or two as a sample of the whole.

Probably the favorite idea, that the negro race is stamped with inferiority, contains as much real argument in support of slavery, as any thing alleged by its advocates. But this, to have the slightest effect, must be carried to the extent of denying the humanity of negroes — an extent reached, to be sure, by the slave system, in its practical treatment of the slave, but never in its laws. The slave code recognizes the elements of man in the negro, and hence takes pains to extinguish those elements. The laws against slaves are evidently not laws against brutes. Rationality and manhood are always implied in the exactions imposed on the negro, and he is required not to exercise these qualities of his nature further or otherwise than may promote the interest of his master. In short, the law, finding the negro, unfortunately, a man, bids him divest himself of manhood, as far as he conveniently can, and identify himself with the brute. This contradiction, then, everywhere appears among slave-holders: they regard the negro as man, and not man. How they can reconcile the contradiction, the world has yet to learn. If we admit the humanity of the negro, all attempts to defend slavery sink at once into contempt. His very weakness and dullness become his protection, among all honorable men. He stands exempted from abuse by the same law which exempts women and children, the sick and the lame, the aged and the insane, from injury. Their want of equal strength has made it dishonorable in the extreme, to prey upon them, or even not to defend them to the utmost of our power. If the negro is really inferior to the white man, either mentally or physically, how despicable in us to take advantage of this, his weakness, and strip him of all his God-given rights! But the assumption of inferiority is altogether gratuitous and improbable. If he is inferior, the fact remains to be proved. We will not insist on this, however, as, if it could be made out, the whole effect would be to enhance our obligations to the colored race, and to throw around them a tenderness and a shield, which, as equals, they have no right to claim.

Founded on this idea of inferiority, is the kindred notion, that the negro is incapable of self-government and of self-maintenance. Were it true that he is too imbecile to discharge the duties of citizenship, this fact, as above intimated, would only throw him more fully upon the charity of the white man. It would not render him the prey of his more intelligent brethren, but an object of still tenderer care.

Another argument, deemed of great weight, is, an alleged forfeiture of all right to freedom, on the part of the slave. Just how this forfeiture occurred, we are not told, but, if we will believe slave-owners, it most certainly exists. The vagueness of such a pretension might well excuse us from all attempts to investigate it; but it may not be best to take advantage of this circumstance. If there has arisen any loss of natural rights to the slave, from any source, that source must be known. Such an alienation could only be the effect of law, and of law made by a competent authority. But when was such a law made by the God of nature? Plainly, the record of it is wanting. Still, if a law, working such disqualification, be allowed to exist, when and how was it violated? These are questions all important to the argument, and if neither the law nor its violation can be shown definitely, the alleged forfeiture vanishes,

"Like the baseless fabric of a vision."

Yet, the fact of such a loss of original rights, is pertinaciously maintained, though no one has ever been absurd enough to profess a belief in the necessary antecedents. There is, indeed, one circumstance which seems to say, that the existence of such a law is an admitted fact, namely, the curse pronounced upon Canaan. Noah said, "cursed be Canaan; a servant of servants shall he be unto his brethren." But to make this available, it must be shown: 1. That the negroes are descendants of Canaan. 2. That this passage is a command or decree, and not a mere prediction. 3. That to be "a servant of servants," means chattel slavery. Until this is done, the passage cannot be applied to the use above specified.

The only further argument that I shall notice, is the plenary power of the civil law to dispose of the natural rights of man. It is claimed that what the law makes property, is property—that in the dispensation of God, to civil government is given full authority to set up and to put down, to destroy or to preserve the rights of man. This claim makes negro slavery only a contingent affair, poised wholly upon the will of the dominant power. The fallacy of such an assumption is very obvious. If human law may thus interfere with the Divine economy, it may do any one, or all, of fifty other things, equally pernicious. That is, the power which can set aside, without cause, one of our natural rights, can set them all aside without cause. This would be to make government, not the guardian and conservator of human rights, but the ruthless destroyer of them. It would put life and all its interests under the control of an irresponsible and unimprovable institution. However consonant with justice such a view of government may be to those who hold slaves, it is to others too manifestly absurd to require the slightest refutation. Such an enormous engine of tyranny and oppression, as would be the civil law, if this were its true exposition, needs only to be known in order to be detested by all upright minds. Besides, it is a sheer begging of the question. There is no evidence that human law has, or can have, any power of this kind. If men are allowed to assume that law may do whatever it pleases, or in other words, that law-makers are under no restraints, then indeed the case is settled. But, as all men, except those in power, deny the existence of such authority, we are bound to reject the pretension, as insult added to injury—as an attempt to cover up fraud by an impudent fiction.

This miserable subterfuge, which constitutes the very animus of Hobbes' political writings, has lately been revived and pressed into service by certain divines, who favor the fugitive slave law. Dr. Lord may be taken as the representative of this class. His doctrine he states in the following words:

"In regard to his own worship, and the manner in which we are to approach Him, the Supreme Governor has given full and minute directions. He has revealed himself, his attributes, and the great principles of his government, which constitute the doctrines of Christianity, and has conferred upon no human authority the right to interfere, by adding to or taking from them. In all things that belong to himself, God exercises sole and absolute jurisdiction, and has, in regard to them, appointed no inferior or delegated authority.

"Governments have jurisdiction over men in all affairs which belong peculiarly to the present life; in all the temporal relations which bind societies, communities, and families together, in respect to all rights of person and property, and their enforcement by penalties. General rules are indeed laid down in the Scriptures for the regulation of human conduct, but God has ordained the 'powers that be' to appoint their own municipal laws, to regulate and enforce existing relations, and to execute judgment upon offenders, under such form of administration as shall be suitable to the circumstances of the people, and chosen by themselves.

"We take the ground, that the action of civil governments, within their appropriate jurisdiction, is final and conclusive upon the citizen: and that to plead a higher law to justify disobedience to a human law, the subject matter of which is within the cognizance of the State, is to reject the authority of God himself, who has committed to governments the power and authority which they exercise in civil affairs."

These extracts contain two assumptions. 1. That the supremacy of the Divine law is confined to things purely religious, or what relates directly to the worship and service of God himself. 2. That governments have, in their particular sphere, unrestricted authority over men. Both assumptions are false, as may be easily shown. In reference to the first, it is sufficient to say that there is no evidence whatever of any such limitation of the Divine supremacy. It is indeed true, that the law of God is supreme in matters of worship, but this is not the whole truth, for his law has the same supremacy in relation to every thing else. The second position is equally untenable. The simple fact that civil government is a Divine institution, does not in the least prove that there is no restriction upon it. Governments are not left to do right or wrong, just as they may choose, but they are bound to do right, and only right. They may do wrong, but they must do it on their own authority, for God never gives authority to do wrong. Hence, if governments do wrong they do it on their own responsibility, and without that authority which renders their acts obligatory when they do right. The right to determine what is the character of governmental requirements, is always with the individual, and not with the government. God requires man always to do right, and if all the governments of the earth should combine to force him to sin, he is bound to resist them, even unto death. It is a most ridiculous supposition, that God should command us "to do to others as we would that they should do unto us," and then subject us to the authority of a Congressional decree which exactly reverses his own command. Dr. Lord's hypothetical distribution of supremacy, is a fiction of his own brain, and derives not the slightest support from Scripture, or from common sense.

Such reasoning has not even the small merit of plausibility. It is instinctively rejected by every sound mind. Suppose that government, to which the right of capital punishment clearly appertains, should, without any alleged reason, order every tenth citizen to be hung, would any man—*could* any man, deem it his duty to obey such a command? Not unless he was willing to incur the guilt of murder. Thus, in spite of thrones, are governments held in check by the higher law of common sense, as well as by revelation.

I have now given a specimen of the reasons—if reasons they may be called—on which this gigantic system of abuse rests. It will be perceived at once, that defence is utterly impossible. To argue in support of such a system is to burlesque it; the prudent will generally choose to rest their cause on prescription, rather than venture a defence, where every argument must inevitably be a mockery of truth and common sense. This was seen by the celebrated Montesquieu, more than a century ago, and long before any effort was made for the abolition of the slave trade. This eminent author proffers the following ironical defence of the system:

"Were I to vindicate our right to make slaves of the negroes, these should be my arguments:

"The Europeans, having extirpated the Americans, were obliged to make slaves of the Africans, for clearing such vast tracts of land.

"Sugar would be too dear, if the plants which produce it were cultivated by any other than slaves.

"These creatures are all over black, and with such a flat nose, that they can scarcely be pitied.

"It is hardly to be believed that God, who is a wise being, should place a soul, especially a good soul, in such a black, ugly body.

"It is so natural to look upon color as the criterion of human nature, that the Asiatics, among whom eunuchs are employed, always deprive the blacks of their resemblance to us, by a more opprobrious distinction.

"The color of the skin may be determined by that of the hair, which, among the Egyptians, the best philosophers in the world, was of such importance, that they put to death all the red haired men who fell into their hands.

"The negroes prefer a glass necklace to that gold which polite nations so highly value: can there be a greater proof of their wanting common sense?

"It is impossible for us to suppose these creatures to be men, because, allowing them to be men, a suspicion would follow, that we ourselves are not Christians.

"Weak minds exaggerate too much the wrong done to the Africans. For were the case as they state it, would the European powers, who make so many needless conventions among themselves, have failed to make a general one in behalf of humanity and compassion?"—*Spirit of Laws: b. 15, ch. 5.*

A zealous and able advocate of slavery might make a less ludicrous defence, but he could not make a more just and truthful one, because vice cannot be defended.

CHAPTER XII.

GOVERNMENT AND RELIGION SUBVERSIVE OF SLAVERY.

I HAVE shown that civil government and Christianity are incompatible with slavery; my object now is, to show that the obligation to maintain these institutions, is an obligation to extirpate slavery. The simple fact of incompatibility, does, in itself, ensure the destruction of slavery, for government and religion cannot co-exist with this fearful antagonist principle. But the duty of extending the former, necessarily inhibits and excludes the latter. It brings opposite elements into conflict, and renders it indispensable that wrong should give place to right. The obligation to maintain government, is an obligation to maintain the rights of the governed. Slavery and government are, therefore, inimical. But, it may be said, that slavery implies government, and we concede the fact, although the concession amounts to nothing. Such government as slavery implies, is a curse, and not a blessing; but the government which God has ordained, and which alone is lawful, is a blessing, and not a curse.

Its design is to uphold the natural rights of man, and especially to protect the weaker members of society against injuries from those who are stronger, or viciously disposed. This obvious intent of civil law, is wholly lost sight of, in the infamous system of slavery. Instead of conserving the liberty of the African, government robs him of every vestige of natural or acquired right, and dooms to the most abject servitude, both him and his posterity, down to the latest generation. It is not possible for a beneficent institution to inflict such a gross outrage as this. And we are constained to hold the government administered by slave-holders, as mere tyranny. It is not government, in any proper sense of the term; it is tyrannical usurpation, operating where, and only where, government has been overthrown.

The extirpation of slavery is, then, not optional with patriotism; it is a work that must be taken in hand by all who would preserve the existence of civil government, and particularly by all those who aim to extend the blessings of social order. Accordingly, we find all upheavings of the masses—all political revolution and resistance to governmental abuses, connected with a recognition of original and imprescriptible rights. Men feel that they should be treated as men; and because they are not so treated, they renounce and crush—but not so frequently as they should—the iniquitous usurpation of tyrants. All this is but an instinctive yearning for a good which civil establishments ought always

to afford, but which is too often prevented by wicked men, who prostitute them to their own aggrandizement.

To charge those who oppose slavery with being enemies of government, and with anarchical designs, is the grossest injustice. Tyranny is the only anarchy, and tyrants are the only anarchists. These break down civil law, and subvert government; these, by the mere wantonness of power, strip men of their rights, without even the forms of justice. For slave-holders and other tyrants to complain of seditious or treasonable conduct, on the part of anti-slavery men, is most ridiculous affectation—most insulting malignity. The old fable says, that the wolf and the lamb were drinking together, out of the same stream, but the lamb, though farthest down the stream, was accused by the wolf, of roiling the water! Surely, nothing but this wolfish propensity can induce any one to charge civil disturbance upon those who only seek to break the chains of the slave, and restore to him his inalienable rights. The real disturber of the peace, is he who took away these rights—not he that brings them back. Humanity has a right to replevy the sacred treasure of personal liberty, and none but those who have feloniously seized it, will ever complain.

Every attempt to administer justice in a slave state, must stand rebuked by those mute, uncomplaining objects, who have been struck dumb by one vast act of oppression. Why shall there be courts of justice among those who have scouted all justice? "Thou that preachest a man should not steal, dost thou steal?" As slavery is the vilest of robbery, and the most enormous injustice which man can possibly commit, it would seem that those who practice it should never profess attachment to the principles of equity, or evince any respect for those rules by which justice is administered among upright men.

But however great may be the antagonism between government and slavery, it is much less than that between religion and slavery. The whole substance of religion is utterly destroyed by slavery; not a single virtue does it leave untouched. Christianity, for instance, teaches justice and even kindness towards all men, not excepting our enemies; but slavery reverses this, by denying either justice or kindness to the colored man. Slavery strips him of his manhood, and not only converts him into a brute, but fixes his market value, and holds him for sale with other articles of commerce. No apology can be made for such an audacious crime—none was ever attempted that did not enhance the guilt of him who made it. The usual sophistries with which the case has been met, have had too much indulgence shown them. Wrong so monstrous, is always premeditated, and to defend it, is to purposely mislead. In like manner we might adduce every virtue enjoined by the gospel, and the system of slavery would show itself the implacable enemy of them all. This is emphatically true of those virtues which, from their being less spiritual, are more akin to the duties enjoined by the civil law; but the difference is still greater in the high department of faith, where benevolence and spirituality give such vast expansion to active goodness. Naked justice and simple kindness fall almost infinitely below the spotless sanctity and burning charity peculiar to the kingdom of God. Now, if slavery is the very opposite of common justice, how satanical must it appear, when contrasted with this exalted purity! The man, whose heart is pervaded by this heavenly virtue, is so far from enslaving his brother man, that he would himself wear the chains, rather than put them on the negro.

> "I would not have a slave to till my ground,
> To carry me, to fan me while I sleep,
> And tremble when I wake, for all the wealth
> That sinews, bought and sold, have ever earned.
> No: dear as freedom is, and in my heart's
> Just estimation prized above all price,
> I had much rather be myself the slave,
> And wear the bonds, than fasten them on him."—*Task.*

A religion that breathes such moral excellence, can never have any affinity with slavery—can neither adopt it, nor consecrate it, nor tolerate it. Such light can have no fellowship with such darkness. And the duty of spreading this religion, involes unceasing warfare against the slave system. We cannot teach men to keep the law of God, without teaching them to break the slave law. Nor may we teach them merely to break the slave law—they must be made to abhor it, and fly from it as they would from hell itself. Religion is, in short, a total disqualification for slave-holding; it incapacitates men for such wickedness; their natures become too refined, too upright, for such enormities. As slavery is vice, its extirpation must result from the prevalence of virtue—that is, a pure religion. No other effect can be anticipated, for no other is possible—religion must either extirpate sin, or itself be extirpated by sin. All Christians are, therefore, necessarily opposed to slavery, and, so far as they have any evangelical goodness, actively engaged in the work of emancipation. And the war now going on against slavery, is only the kingdom of Christ arraying itself against antichrist.

CHAPTER XIII.

CAPACITY OF SLAVES FOR CIVIL GOVERNMENT.

Having noticed (chap. xi.) the usual objections to emancipation, particularly those founded on the alleged inferiority of the African race, and on their supposed incapacity for self-government, I shall now attempt to show, not as in the aforesaid chapter, that these things, if true, constitute no apology for slavery — but that they are totally false assumptions. Tyrants have always assigned as the reason for their usurpations, that the people were incompetent to govern themselves. This charge of incompetency is a gross and willful imposture. It is a pretext that can hardly be said to have the poor merit of plausibility. What great strength of mind or of body have rulers ever exhibited above the people whom they ruled? Had Nero more capacity for civil government than any other man in the Roman empire? Or, rather, could any other man in Rome or out of Rome have governed worse? This course of reasoning is applicable to all who have swayed the rod of empire, and in too many instances with precisely the same result. Emperors, kings, and governors, instead of being wiser, or better, or more competent in any respect for the duties of government, than their subjects, have too generally been notorious for depravity and imbecility—have sunk far below the average level of virtue in their own dominions, and proved a curse, instead of blessing, to those whom they governed. Why then this idle talk of the necessity, of superior abilities in those who govern? And why affirm so unhesitatingly, that even the lowest in the scale of intelligence and virtue are not capable of government? Rulers have generally been quite as ignorant and debased, as the people from among whom they were taken and placed in authority. The idea that wisdom centres in public authority, or in men who are accidentally at the head of political affairs, is very foolish; it implies a total ignorance of the true nature of civil government. Office-holders, whether kings, or governors, or legislators, are only servants of the public, and have no other means of becoming capable of exercising civil authority, than have those who employ them—those who give them all their power. The people are proprietors, under God, of civil institutions, and it is extremely absurd to suppose that they are not capable of managing their own affairs. For rulers to claim superior fitness, is proof of dishonesty; it shows that there is treachery, and that the charge of incompetency serves only to conceal the fraud.

Ignorance is a term which must be applied to slaves with great care. The slave is a man, and man cannot be so ignorant as to be incapable of civil government. A brute is thus ignorant, because he is a brute; God did not give him the faculties necessary to civil order, nor can he ever acquire them. But to man, these faculties are given by his Creator; and they belong inalienably to his constitution. He has these powers as he has life—not by education and custom, but by the hand of God, which formed him a rational creature. The attempt to put him in the category of brutes, merely because he has not undergone a long course of training in republican forms, is either a very stupid blunder, or a dastardly piece of injustice.

But it may be said that slaves are illiterate, and therefore disqualified for civil duties, inasmuch as such duties require a knowledge of written law. This argument takes for granted that literature is essential to virtue; but the history of the world shows quite the contrary. Many who could not read, have proved themselves capable of the noblest deeds, while many others, though possessed of learning, have exhibited nothing but meanness. It is altogether a mistake to suppose that literature, in any shape or degree, is indispensable to freedom. As well might we deem it indispensable to the digestion of food, or the circulation of the blood. Letters are only a convenience, invented by man, but liberty is an element of his nature, derived from the Creating hand. Not to have the former, is to lack an important branch of education; not to have the latter, is to be less than man: the one is non-improvement; the other, mutilation.

With like inconsistency, it has been pretended that freedom can be conferred only by degrees—that liberty should be only gradually introduced among the oppressed. We might waive all remarks here, as even gradual emancipation is never proposed by slave-holders. But the question has its interest, since there are emancipationists who are horror struck at the thought of immediate enfranchisement. They would have the chains of the slave broken, link by link, and so slowly that an age would hardly suffice to liberate him. And all this, from an erroneous notion that enduring the misfortunes and abuses of a vile tyranny, is the best preparation for liberty. If preparation is necessary, in order to freedom, most certainly it will have to be found in something besides chattel slavery. How can the complete annihilation of political rights and immunities, fit people for the proper use of such rights and immunities? As well put out a man's eyes to help his vision, or cut off his feet to quicken his pace. We deny, however, that any preparation is necessary. Liberty being the birth-right of man, the natural and normal condition of his existence, all the preparation he needs for its enjoyment is born with him. He gets his fitness for liberty, as he gets his hands and his feet—not by education, but by inheritance. It is born with him, and constitutes a part of his being. We may see by the family relation, what is demanded in the weakest condition of human nature. Children require parental control, and so may very ignorant adults; but there is nothing in the government of a family analogous to slavery. No child is subject to sale, no right which can safely be exercised is withheld, and the whole course of discipline and restraint is one of tenderness. But what is more, the disabilities of children are temporary; as soon as they attain to a given age, the law confers on them whatever was withheld during minority. If the boon of citizenship thus inured to the slave, he would have all the preparation for liberty which the nature of man can be supposed to require. We do not, however, regard the minority of children as intended merely to prepare them for the duties and immunities of civil life. Their physical helplessness, which for several years is such that they would perish, if left to themselves, is the grand reason why they are placed under parental care. Other advantages grow out of this dependence, and the child doubtless finds in the family authority milder and better control than could be administered by the State.

It is clear, therefore, that the gradual emancipation of adults, finds no support from the gradual emancipation, if such it may be called, of children. The latter are physically and mentally incompetent to the task of life; they must be protected and cherished by others, till nature brings them to sufficient maturity, to render them independent. This maturity the adult slave has already gained, and the law should at once enfranchise him. There is, moreover, this difference: in the case of children, privileges are only held in abeyance—not extinguished. The child is an heir, is as fully protected from injury as the adult, and no right can be taken from him. On the contrary, the rights of the slave are totally destroyed, and this, irrespective of age, or physical or mental condition.

That ignorant people are not fitted for self-government, or rather, for civil freedom, is a notion long current in certain quarters, and for very obvious reasons. It is the interest of rulers to create this impression, that their services may be the more esteemed. Such a plea serves well as an excuse for usurpation. Dynasties would soon tumble into ruins, but for this aspersion of human capacity. Were it understood that people—any people, even the most ignorant—could dispense with tyranny and suffer no harm, where would be the support of unrighteous authority? Rulers would sink into servants; they would govern for the people, and not for themselves. This deception is based, in part, on the idea that freedom requires unusual ability. It has come to be a prevalent opinion, that a good government is fit only for the best of people—the most wise, intelligent and virtuous. But on this principle, it might be maintained that bad children should have bad parents, or that sick people should have worse treatment than those in health. Surely, if a difference is to be made, humanity requires that the burden should not be thrown upon the weak—that a bad government should not be inflicted on those who have the least skill in political affairs. If good government is wanted any where, it is among the ignorant and the vile. The end of civil institutions is protection; but protection oppresses no one. To secure the rights of individuals, in a bad state of society, may require greater efficiency and care in government; yet, this can never be a reason for tyranny, because tyranny is not protection, and, therefore, not the object which government has in view.

Civil law is to man, as any other essential want of his nature. He needs government just as he needs food, and there is no more incapacity in him for one of these things than for the other; nor is there any necessity that his wants, in either case, should be supplied with what is deteriorated and vile. He can endure the depravation of food, quite as well as the depravation of government. The whole history of mankind shows that tyranny can evolve nothing but tyranny—that governmental evils have no tendency to self-correction, and that the elevation of the slave cannot be promoted by even his temporary subjection to despotism. Oppression may lead to revolution, and often does, but it has not the slightest power to develope fitness for liberty. It may indeed generate a deep abhorrence of tyranny, and thus increase the love of freedom; still, as this abhorrence and this love are instinctive traits of man, they scarcely need such an unnatural expansion. The desire for liberty, like the desire for justice, or food, or health, is naturally strong enough, and nothing is gained by the artificial stimulus consequent upon misgovernment. Political freedom is only political justice, and all men are as ready for this description of justice, as for any other. It will be as harmless to give them full freedom, as it would be to give them full light for the eye, or full air for the lungs, or full pay for honest dues.

The following remarks are so pertinent to the general question now under consideration, that I cannot deny myself the pleasure of inserting them.

"The next fallacy is, that freedom should follow, but never lead, a true civilization; that it is the crown and capital, but not the base. It is an axiom with us, that we, only, are fit for liberty. It seems to be supposed that a despotism has some secret nourishment of liberty in it, and that after a certain time, free institutions will result from it. What evidence of progress have we in China and Japan? Why were not Persia and the old monarchies gradually prepared for free institutions? Because despotism dwarfs men—necessarily dwarfs them, and lies on them as a blight and canker. When we are told, therefore, to wait before we assist other nations, let us inquire what we are waiting upon? We are waiting until despotism has done its perfect work—until it has slain the hope and vitality of the oppressed. Do you say that education is favored by despotism. Yes, and let China, Austria, and storied Italy answer what are the results of art, literature and scholarship in the matter of emancipation. The study and the cell make the artist and scholar free, but they give him liberty, too often misused to the oppression of his fellows. They are not apt to encourage that state of things which interferes with their seclusion. Literature and art have not been the friends of liberty, but the most obsequious servants of absolutism. Nor does popular education do much more. It may make only a race of curious dreamers, rather than of energetic men. What is education but a tool, which depends for its value upon the hand that holds it? Reading and writing cannot conjure intelligence into humanity or out of it. Pigs may be taught to read. Education is not education when it leaves the scholar passive. The old schoolmen were only elaborately ignorant, differing from other men as a parrot which can talk differs from one which cannot. He who speaks no senseat all in several languages, will pass for more than he who speaks solid sense in only one. Popular education owes its value to a roused intelligence. Our institutions are our educators. I heard Kossuth say, when he meant the universal people, the university of the people. Yes, freedom is that, it is the university of the people. So it is not our religious education that fosters our love of liberty, but it is liberty which fosters the Church. In despotic lands is religion always begetting freedom? Is the bench of Bishops in England perpetually presenting schemes of progress and reform? Issachar is a strong ass, bending between two burdens—the taxing State and the grinding Church. In America, the clergy are free and preach liberty, because the spirit of the country allows it. Liberty is the first interest of a nation. It sets humanity going, and keeps it going. The other influences are regulating, this is conservative. The prosperity of this country is owing to the wonderful activity of human faculties here.

"What, then, ought to be our hope, prayer and act for other nations? While they are content with death, ought we to be content for them? While we acknowledge that liberty alone is the life of the race, that it, only, underlies and inspires prosperity—what shall we do and say? Is the breaking of this bastile of despotism to make no more noise than the breaking of an egg for breakfast? Is order to be purchased at every price? Are nations lying like lambs, and tyrants hanging over them like butchers, to excite no word and no act from us, because the slaughter-house is not on our own shores? Nothing but liberty can save a nation from a broken heart and moral death. We must expect disorder from the resurrection of nations. Poor, old, bed-ridden humanity may break the furniture of her chamber when she begins to walk—when she escapes from the nurses who have been keeping her ill, that they might more conveniently consume her estate. But she must forth, she has a right to walk, although every step should be an earthquake,—although she tumble over thrones and privileges as she advances."—Rev. H. W. BELLOWS, (*recent lecture at the Tabernacle, N. Y.*)

CHAPTER XIV.

THE FUGITIVE SLAVE LAW.

This law, so justly offensive to the free states, and so exactly in harmony with the slave states, is only a further development of that gigantic system of robbery, which the federal government has always tolerated, and often encouraged. It was natural that slave-holders should wish to do everywhere what they do where slavery is allowed, and hence, they spare no pains to secure the passage of such laws, by Congress, as will enable them to recover fugitive slaves in the most summary manner. In substance, the fugitive slave law is like all other slave laws; it is characterized by the same total disregard of personal rights and sheer contempt for humanity. It is not more cruel than the ordinary legislation of slave states, nor is it less so; and had it taken place in slave territory—had its operation been confined to people already accustomed to slave-holding—it would have excited no unfavorable remark. But when it is attempted to transfer a portion of the slave law to free states, and make it operative there, nothing but the most absolute coercion can render the experiment successful. How far such coercion is available, remains to be seen.

The law was introduced into Congress and passed by that body, on the basis of the constitution. The following is the clause on which this master-piece of legislation rests:

> "No person held to service or labor in one state, under the laws thereof, escaping into another, shall, in consequence of any law or regulation therein, be discharged from such labor; but shall be delivered up on claim of the party to whom such labor or service may be due."—*Const. U. S. A.: art. 1, sec.* 2.

Here we evidently have a compromise. The non-slave-holding states are forbidden to make any law emancipating such slaves as flee from the slave states. But for this protective clause in the constitution, the free states would, unquestionably, have made every African free on entering their limits. Whether the compromise is, in itself, a violation of human rights, and whether it makes the general government, to all intents and purposes, a slave-holding power, are points on which there is some difference of opinion. From the circumstances of the case, as well as from the very cautious and sparing reference to slavery in the constitution, I judge that there was no intention to assume the guilt or to foster the institution of slavery. Still, all men must regret the existence of such a compromise, as it certainly tolerates, if it does not sanction slavery.

In forming a confederacy out of independent states, part of them averse to the continuance of slavery and part otherwise, it became necessary to make some concessions; but philanthropists have always deplored that such a concession as this was demanded, or admitted. It was purchasing union at too costly a rate. The specific objections to the fugitive slave law, which has grown out of this unfortunate clause, are as follows:

It is unconstitutional.

That the constitution gives to the slave-holder a right to recover his absconding slave, is beyond dispute. No state may annul the claim of the master, or prevent his seizing his slave wherever he can find him. The sympathies of freemen are held in check, so far as to refrain from all emancipating legislation in aid of the fugitive. This is the extent of the compromise, and thus far the supervision of Congress might lawfully extend, according to the terms of the national compact. All laws for the emancipation, concealment, or non-release of fugitive slaves, were prohibited by the constitution, and might be pronounced null and void by the United States Judiciary. Had Congress done no more than this, the rights of freemen would have remained intact, save in the check put upon the active exercise of that benevolence which is due to the oppressed. But the present fugitive slave law creates a special court, and clothes that court with special and unprecedented powers, for the sole purpose of accommodating slave-holders, by effecting a speedy reclamation of alleged fugitives. It is needless to say that the language of the constitution, on which this extraordinary enactment depends, gives no authority to Congress to institute any court whatever; much less does it authorize the establishment of such tribunals as now decide the fate of those whom slave-holders claim as their property.

Freemen are liable to be enslaved.

It is true that the innocent are always liable to be ensnared, by laws intended only for the guilty, but the danger in this instance is pre-eminent and needless. Evidence, exceedingly scant, and drawn from remote sources, and even from questionable persons, is allowed to fix the doom of a man forever, and all his children after him. The jury—that palladium of legal rights—is dispensed with, as though it were not safe to adjudicate claims to property consisting in man, with the same care that is necessary when the property in dispute is a horse! The constitution, in allowing the slave-holder to reclaim his slave, cannot be understood as waiving the ordinary forms of justice, by which human rights are settled. Why such despatch in a matter of such inconceivable importance to one of the parties litigant? Even conceding that the slave, though a man, can never be entitled to the rights of man, why shall other men—the free-born blacks, who are not slaves, and never were — be subjected to this imminent peril? The law exposes every colored man in the free states to the rapacity of kidnappers. Under the pretence of accelerating the reclamation of fugitives, it breaks down all the barriers of freedom, and consigns the unoffending freeman to hopeless bondage. This would be quite consistent in a slave state, where all colored men are considered lawful prey; but it is monstrous in a state where personal rights are sacred, whatever may be the complexion of the skin.

It exacts of freemen a service which they cannot conscientiously render.

The law not only secures the rendition of slaves, but compels northern men to lend themselves as instruments in this abominable work. Thus, a man who abhors slavery as he does murder, must pay a fine, and perhaps suffer imprisonment, or assist the proper authorities in remanding the fugitive to his chains. The constitution — sadly as it compromises — has nothing of this; it barely gives the slave-owner permission to recover, by such means as may be in his power, the man who flees from him. But by this regulation, men who scorn the unholy business of slave-holding and slave-catching, are forced to engage in it, or openly resist the law and incur its penalties. Surely, it was enough that all the generous and humane feelings of freemen should be stifled, or restricted to a merely faithful investigation of the slave-holder's claim, without this necessity of defiling themselves, by assisting to manacle one whose right to liberty is at least as good as their own, and whose misfortunes commend him so powerfully to every philanthropic mind. Let men who believe it right to rob the colored man, do this work if they will, but let no other man be compelled to aid them in the crime.

It makes the free states slave hunting-ground.

Not content with denying all aid to the slave, this law makes him an object to be sought with avidity through every free state in the Union. It converts the non-slave-holding states into a vast theatre for slave-catching. Africa itself could hardly afford better facilities. Any man at the South who may wish to increase his slave population, has only to make an incursion upon the North, and seize negroes wherever he meets them. This done, the smothered, summary, mock trial which follows, affords but a slight obstacle to success. Never had kidnapping greater conveniences; never had avarice, lust, and cruelty, a better chance to prey upon the innocent and the helpless. The free colored people of the North are literally given up to destruction, and the whole country is made a recruiting ground for slavery. A business—slave-importing—which the federal government justly treats as piracy, when carried on between Africa and this country, is sanctioned and vindicated on the soil of every free republican state. To seize, or even to purchase slaves in a foreign land, and bring them home, is death; but they may be seized and imported, by government authority, and at government expense, too, from any neighboring state in the Union. This is the climax of horrors.

The expense of recovering slaves is unjustly thrown upon the national treasury.

It would be exceedingly wrong in a slave-holding state to make the treasury sustain such a burden, unless all were slave-holders, and had an equal interest in the re-capture of fugitives. But the wrong is greatly enhanced when the expense devolves on the general government, whose revenues are chiefly derived from non-slave-holding states. The constitution gives no intimation of such an expenditure, and we cannot believe that either the framers of that instrument, or the people who adopted it, would have consented to such an arrangement. As well might the cost of returning stray cattle or horses be charged to the nation. Slaves are held as personal property, and it was quite enough that the free states should be prohibited the exercise of hospitality towards them, without being compelled to share in the expense of their re-enslavement. Yes, it was enough that they must witness the hunting of slaves in their midst, and on their own free soil, without being obliged to defray the cost of such an infamous transaction.

It makes the United States a slave-holding nation. The constitution does but tolerate slavery, whereas the fugitive slave law endorses and approves it. The former was only a compromise measure, in which nothing was granted that could be withheld; the latter is a voluntary grant of every thing that could be granted. The latter, we are aware, was intended as a compromise, but it is not so much a compromise as a surrender. It yields to the slave-catcher all that the most unbounded cruelty and insatiate avarice could demand. It takes from the African race all humanity, in all parts of the nation, and makes freemen every where the servile tools of slaveocratic injustice. Until this infamous concession, the non-slave-holder might regard himself as free from all positive connection with slavery. Neither his hands nor his money were at the command of the slave-holder; but under this law, no man is exempt. Slave-catching has become a national business, and every man is compelled to engage in it. Thus quickly has the bare permission to re-capture fugitive slaves among us, ripened into an obligation to do this work ourselves.

These are the principal features of this strange piece of legislation. We have no wish to exaggerate its defects, and certainly they are beyond apology. The studied contempt with which it treats the freemen of the North, could hardly have been greater, and is unusual; but its persevering inhumanity to the negro is only characteristic, and not excessive beyond precedent. Towards him, legislation long since did its worst; there was no new degree of oppression to be reached; his rights had all been utterly swept away before. Of course, this must be understood of the slave states, as the national government, though crippled by compromise, had not, until the enactment of this law, arrayed itself on the side of the oppressor. The African, when not a slave, was treated, if not like other men, yet like a human being—like one to whose interests the law was not wholly indifferent—like one who was to be protected, rather than destroyed by vengeful statutes.

We are very sorry the constitution contains any thing that can, in the remotest degree, be pressed into this slave-catching business. When men have had the courage and adroitness to throw off their chains, they certainly ought to meet, at the hands of a government which began its own career by announcing "that all men are created equal," something better than a re-enslavement. But the constitution is not justly chargeable with the present fugitive slave law. The former is to the latter, as

"Hyperion to a Satyr."

There neither is, nor can be, any sort of resemblance between the two, except that both are entities. Our chary constitution, too scrupulous and sensitive to pollute itself with even the word slavery, cannot, with decency, be made responsible for the grand kidnapping law under which slave-holders are now rioting.

Surely there is nothing in it that forbids a trial by jury, or that mulcts with heavy damages men who cannot conscientiously engage in slave-catching—nothing that makes the general government pay all expenses of returning fugitives, or that obligates it to create a special court, and to endow that court with dangerous powers, for the re-capture of slaves. Simply requiring a state not to pass a law enfranchising the slave who comes within its bounds, and requiring further, that the fugitive shall be given up, cannot, without the greatest violence, be construed into such a disgraceful and ruinous thing as is the fugitive slave law. We have a law requiring prisoners and felons who have escaped to other states, to be given up on the requisition of the governor; but the slave is not dignified with any form of requisition—he is prosecuted and taken back with less ceremony than a common felon. And be it remembered, that all free colored men, yes, and all free white men, are every hour exposed to this summary process. The fugitive slave law knows nothing of color: it takes effect on "persons held to labor," be they white or black, and tries them with whatever of evidence may chance to be at hand.

Congress was supporting the constitution at a strange rate, when it receded more than two centuries and made this fugitive law. A little more such support, and our political fabric will tumble into chaos. Such bungling is too horrible for endurance; and it is especially insupportable when charged upon the patriotic fathers of the republic—men who abolished the slave trade, and who did all in their power to abolish slavery at home.

Some additional features of this law, together with its practical workings, are very forcibly expressed in the following extract:

"There are reasons intrinsic to the bill, that will make it a loathing, and will, when it comes to be fully known, make it, we believe, the most odious act with which flagitious legislation ever abused public confidence.

"One would have thought that an end so atrocious as this legal slave trade—as much worse than African, as it is worse to steal a man conscious of worth and eager for liberty, than it would be to steal a wild savage, ignorant of rights and dignities, should have been sought in the most gentle and unobtrusive ways. But no. It breaks in upon the community like a hyena. It prostrates the great barriers which civilization has erected about individual rights—the habeas corpus act, the right of trial by jury, and often practically the right to confront one's accusers. That nothing might be wanting to render an infamous thing consistently infamous throughout, the bill provides a bribe of five dollars to the commissioner for every man tried, and ten for every man convicted! Five dollars for acquittal and twice as much for conviction!

"Here is a government agent, with the powers of a civil court, whose salary depends upon the number of cases he can bring before him, and doubles whenever he convicts the arraigned! Who would go before a court of his country if he knew that the judge had a pecuniary interest in his conviction? And yet the rights and liberties of thousands and thousands of men are, under this bill, to be adjudicated, without trial by jury, without appeal, upon testimony unregulated, save by the judgment of the commissioner, who is made personally and pecuniarily interested in every conviction!

"There is one deep lower yet. If a wretch, endeavoring to escape the fangs of this venomous reptile, this coil of serpents, be aided by a humane man, heavy fines and bonds await such beneficence!

"Ought they to be deemed prudent men or safe guides, who assure the South that such a law will be executed in the North?

"Yet there are some reasons why we, too, rejoice in the execution of this law.

"We are glad, because every slave taken from our midst back to slavey is an appeal to humanity against oppression. It is bringing the abomination of slavery to our very door. We are not obliged now to stretch our eyes across the ocean to Africa, to see men snatched up as they fly from burning villages or captured in war, and shipped for Christian markets. Slave catching may now be pursued in New York, in Boston, in Pittsburgh, in Cincinnati. It requires but two lying witnesses to doom any black man. It required only three hours to convert a respectable, honest, industrious free laborer in our streets into a slave under the plantation lash. When these things are done in the South they get cool before they reach us; but now we are to have slave-hunting, slave-catching and slave-making on our own premises. Is it by such means that the public mind is to be quieted? Is this the way to avoid and allay excitement, of which certain presses have had such dread? Will there be no violence, no bloodshed among those poor fugitives, whose love of liberty is as strong as ours, and who, like us, would sooner die than go into slavery? Are the arguments to which we are to yield our anti-slavery doctrines, irons on honest men's wrists; families broken up — a Hallet at one blow struck out of the catalogue of men, his wife and children left without even the privilege of saying farewell? Are these to be means of grace to all who have agitated the public in the matter of slavery?

"We 'rejoice,' too, that we are spared any further argument against the abominations of the fugitive slave bill. That bill is now pleading against itself. The law doing its work, is the only argument needed for men whose hearts are flesh. While the bill was at Washington it was a mere shadow. It was not possible to make our citizens feel that the public men, whom they revered, could give voice and vote for anything really inimical to liberty. But it is no shadow now. The law stands in our streets — with eye of fire searching every trembling black man; with feet of wind it pursues, and with hands of iron it grasps him. The bill is in our courts. The officers obey it. Judges and commissioners are crouching before it. Slavery has its guardian genius spreading its dragon wings over the bench of justice, and beneath its frown our officials quail and yield? Overawed, they will give up the slave, that is no slave, but of right, in his own blood, and by the blood of Christ, a freeman! It is good for our reflecting men to see these things. We protested against the bill while it was travailing in birth. Our words only brought reproaches. Since then, the thing must come, we are glad; we 'rejoice,' that sober and humane men will deal no longer with an abstraction, but are forced to see a living law feeding on injustice, and spewing blood in our streets.

"We 'rejoice' that men who have tasted of liberty, who

have been made intelligent by it, if sent back to slavery, will not go as they came. They return missionaries, teachers of liberty and escape wherever they go. Put them in prison, put them in coffles, send them in gangs southward; prisons, irons, travel and the biting lash will never obliterate what they have learned. It is a wonderful providence that the South should send their shrewdest slaves to the North, until they have become thoroughly trained to liberty, and then send for them to come back, and spread the infection from plantation to plantation!

"We solemnly appeal to Christians of every name, to all sober and humane men, unwrenched by party feelings, to all that love man, to behold and ponder this iniquity which is done among us! Shall an army of wretched victims, without a crime, unconvicted of wrong, pursuing honest occupations, be sent back to a loathed and detestable slavery? Here is no 'abstract' question. We ask you, shall men now free—shall members of the church—shall children from the school—shall even ministers of the gospel—be sezied, ironed, and in two hours be on the road to a servitude to them worse than death?

"For our own selves, we do not hesitate to say, what every man who has a spark of manhood in him will say with us, that no force should bring *us* into such horrible bondage. Before we would yield ourselves, or go away to linger and long for death, through burning years of injustice, we would die a thousand deaths. Every house should be our fortress; and when fortress and refuge failed us, then our pursuers should release our souls to the hands of God who gave them, before they should degrade them by a living slavery! Who shall deny these feelings and such refuge to a black man?

"With such solemn convictions, no law, impious, infidel

to God and humanity, shall have respect or observance at our hands. We desire no collision with it. We shall not rashly dash upon it. We shall not attempt a rescue, nor interrupt the officers, if they do not interrupt us. We prefer to labor peacefully for its early repeal, meanwhile saving from its merciless jaws as many victims as we can. But in those provisions which respect aid to fugitives, may God do so to us, yea, and more also, if we do not spurn it as we would any other mandate of satan. If in God's Providence, fugitives ask bread or shelter, raiment or conveyance, at our hands, my own children shall lack bread before they; my own flesh shall sting with cold ere they shall lack raiment. I will both shelter them, conceal them, or speed their flight; and while under my shelter, or under my convoy, they shall be to me as my own flesh and blood; and whatsoever defence I would put forth for my own children, that shall these poor, despised and persecuted creatures have in my house or upon the road. The man who shall betray a fellow creature to bondage, who shall obey this law to the peril of his soul, and to the loss of his manhood, were he brother, son or father, shall never pollute my hand with grasp of hideous friendship, or cast his swarthy shadow across my threshold! For such service to those whose helplessness and poverty make them peculiarly God's children, I shall cheerfully take the pains and penalties of this bill. Bonds and fines shall be honors; imprisonment and suffering will be passports to fame, not long to linger! It is a joy and glory to believe that in these sentiments, substantially, the citizens of the North solemnly acquiesce."

That this law has been executed with characteristic atrocity, is evident from the entire series of arrests which have taken place under it. In scarce a singe instance have the proceedings exhibited any thing like a careful and impartial judicial investigation.

REFLECTIONS.

We may well pause, at this stage of the argument. Enough has been exhibited to show the true character of slavery, and of that perverted legislation which upholds it. Can such a catalogue of enormities find any support or countenance among honest men? Especially, can it plead the sanction of Scripture? To ask these questions is to answer them—it being impossible that the heart of man, or the word of God, should approve of such abominations. Either there is no difference between right and wrong—no such thing as virtue—or slavery is a crime of the deepest dye. But moral distinctions are too firmly fixed in man, and in all things around him, not to be seen and recognized. They must be admitted and approved, however painful or strange the evasions that may follow. It is this necessity which has put slavery on its defence—nay, has driven it to the awful extremity of denying the supremacy of God, in his word and works. This antagonism was not of choice—it came unavoidably. Slavery must stand convicted of every offence, or impeach the tribunal before which it was arraigned. It preferred the latter: hence this demonstration against the higher law. Nature having fixed the stamp of humanity upon the negro, would not betray him to the lust and cupidity of the slave-holder, therefore, nature must be repudiated. The Bible, equally unyielding in its impartial distribution of rights, and withal, openly asserting its own superiority to all laws that man can ordain, must, of course, be renounced: not in form, to be sure, but substantially, by a new and flagrant antinomianism. Better so, however, than by any means to have introduced confusion, and thus obscured our moral perceptions. This rejection of the higher law, as unfitted to regulate the government and legislation of slave states, is the homage which vice must ever pay to virtue. This dis-fellowship which slavery seeks, marks its depravity as with a sun-beam.

The question now is, whether we shall continue to endure a system which thus slinks away from the light—which can have no fellowship with goodness—no, not even with God himself, because of his purity. Can the common sense of man tolerate a system so black with abominations that it must flout decency as well as piety? Shall we still legislate against crime, and yet allow this aggregation of all crimes to pass unreproved? It would seem, that the time has come for men who cultivate virtue, and who cherish a righteous repugnance to sin, to gather up the moral force of their souls, and give the world some adequate demonstration of their abhorrence of a system of such extensive and unmitigated wickedness.

How long shall a nation of such exquisite moral refinement, and such jealous regard to political rights as not to endure even a questionable tax, hesitate, when called to decide on the rights of three millions of unoffending citizens? Shall we have the indecency to claim liberty for ourselves, and deny it to others, who are guilty of no crime? That the African is black, must be admitted, but will any one pretend that this is a sufficient reason for depriving him, not only of liberty, in the common acceptation of the term, but of all the rights of humanity? Is the color of the skin what constitutes the difference between man and the brutes? Dare any man attempt to maintain such an absurdity? If not, why then do we adhere so pertinaciously to this unparalleled abuse?

The fact is, this question ought never to have been debated. It is plain, beyond the need of argument. The rights of the African constitute one of those first truths which are to be acknowledged at sight. All who allow to the negro manhood, are bound to allow him the inalienable rights of manhood. Under any ordinary state of things, so plain and palpable a truth could not require even to be stated in order to be approved. The common sense of mankind, when not misled by interest or by education, is always sufficient to induce assent to such a truth, without the formality of argument. But we have fallen upon strange times, and the most sacred rights must either be defended by argument, or be trampled in the dust.

CHAPTER XIV.

CONSTITUTIONS AND COMPROMISES.

But what is more astonishing than any thing else in this history of crime, is the apology so often made for it—slavery is constitutional! The slave laws are traced to the constitutions of the several slaveholding states, and the fugitive slave law is referred to the constitution of the United States, as though the constitutionality of these laws fully justified their atrocity. It surely must be a corrupt fountain that sends forth such poluted streams, and we may well inquire, by what authority any constitution, whether of a single state, or of all the states combined, thus strikes down the liberties of a particular class.

1. If one man's rights may be sacrificed by the constitution, then another's may be, and so on, till all except the usurping few are reduced to vassalage. Let it be granted that a constitution may rightfully be so framed as to enslave one man, or one class of men, and no limit can be assigned to its enslaving power, but the caprice of those by whom it is made. There is no rule for enslaving Africans that will not apply just as well to white men. As

the right to make slaves cannot be conceded without putting every man's liberty in peril, it is fair to assume that no such right now exists, or ever did exist. Such lawless, despotic power was never lodged in human hands.

2. A constitution which reduces any portion of society to slavery, is only an instrument of plunder: it is the work of men combined for robbing. In such cases, law—constitutional law—is wholly perverted, and instead of being a blessing, it becomes the occasion of inexpiable wrongs.

3. To plead such a constitution as an excuse for slavery, is adding insult to injury. The very design for which a constitution, or any vestige of civil law, exists, is defeated. The avowed object of government is protection, and to say that the constitution recognizes slavery, is to say that the very means of liberty have been converted into an engine of oppression. Law, which should ever be not only right, but the guarantee of right, is itself made a crime, and the cause of innumerable crimes.

4. The constitution is only a mere agreement—and in this case an agreement to do wrong. It is quite certain that such agreements or contracts, made by men, depend for their validity upon their rectitude. The mere fact of an arrangement or stipulation, entered into by any number of men, for governmental purposes, does not, in the least, make such an arrangement binding. It may be that the agreement contemplates some horrid crime—as, for

instance, murder—and does any one believe that such an agreement has any binding force?

5. Men have no right to make a constitution which sanctions slavery, and it is the imperative duty of all good men to break it, when made. The right to make laws does not flow from a constitution, for a constitution is itself a law; it is a right which belongs to human nature, and which that nature is bound to exercise with due regard to the eternal principles of rectitude. The fact that a law is constitutional amounts to nothing, unless it is also pure; it must harmonize with the law of God, or be set at naught by all upright men. Wicked laws not only may be broken, but absolutely must be broken; there is no other way to escape the wrath of God. It is not optional with men whether they keep such laws or not; to keep them is death, and not to keep them is the way to life.

We have heard much about the compromises of the constitution, and men have shamelessly asserted that these must be kept at all hazards. So far as such compromises are innocent they may be innocently kept, unless they are so foolish as to amount to a perversion of the common sense which men are always bound to exercise—but no compromise, having for its object the injury or spoliation of any man, or number of men, can be kept for a moment by a Christian. He has no more right to agree with others to strip the negro of his political rights, than he has to enter into a conspiracy against the lives of his fellow-citizens. Still, we are told that the constitution requires it, and therefore, we must catch slaves for the South, just as though such an infamous crime could be made obligatory by a human law. If the constitution requires it, our duty is to spurn the infamous requirement, as we would a command to murder our best friend; and if we have by any means become a party to a wicked compact, which pledges us to the perpetual robbing and degradation of the negro, we are under the most solemn obligations to amend the compact, or renounce it forever. We have a right to make compromises in constitutions, and in any other way we choose, but no man has a right to do wrong—he may not sacrifice another's liberty, nor his own.

The flippancy with which this boasted plea of constitutional obligation has been put forth on all occasions, has made it truly disgusting. It seems to have been entirely forgotten that an agreement to do wrong could have no force—that the constitution must depend upon its character for its authority, and not on the number of men who had consented to it, or the number of bayonets that could be brought to support it. Robbing, perpetrated by whomsoever it may be, is still robbing; nor does the form, the manner, or the instrumentality employed, at all abate the iniquity of the deed. It may be done by a constitution, by a legislative enactment, or by a pistol held to the victims breast; but in either case the wrong is the same. The denationalization of Poland by sovereign princes did not sanctify the act; it was spoliation and robbery, just as much as if it had been done by private individuals.

We have then arrived at this great truth, that men may be guilty of robbing in making a constitution — yes, the very worst kind of robbing. They may plunder the helpless, and consign unborn millions to hopeless servitude. There is, indeed, hardly any other way in which such deep and damning injustice can be perpetrated. If the makers of law — whether constitutional or statute — were exempted from the usual obligations of humanity, and, if their decrees could have any authority apart from justice, then might we appeal to the law as a reason for oppression. But as the case now stands, such an appeal is only offering one wrong as an excuse for an other.

When the fundamental law of the land is proved to be a conspiracy against human rights; when, instead of protecting equally and impartially every human being within its range, it remorselessly and without provocation, delivers up large numbers to irredeemable bondage; then, and in so far, law ceases to be law, and becomes a wanton outrage on society. It is the predominance of brute force, acting on the authority of brute force, and in defiance of the moral law. Dishonesty is none the less dishonesty for assuming the shape of law; the drapery in which it chooses to appear, neither changes its nature nor gives it authority; it is just as detestable and unlawful as if it appeared in its true character.

So much, then, for the boasted and revered compromises of the constitution. They show only that the liberties of men have been shamelessly bartered—that proscription was one of the terms of the compact—that the law-making power, in its highest function, has been guilty of the most aggravated abuse.

The conclusion of the whole matter is this: Before God and all good men, the slave laws are a nullity. Slavery is villainy—"the sum of all villainies"—and CANNOT BE LEGALIZED.

CHAPTER XV.

EFFECTS OF SLAVERY ON THE FREE STATES.

It has been contended by many, that the North has no interest in the question of slavery, and consequently, that northern men should not interfere with what is peculiarly and exclusively a Southern institution. It is time that slave-holders and all others were undeceived on this point. The South may have all the slaves, but they cannot have all the miserable effects of slavery. In many ways the free states are made to share a large part of the evils, which necessarily result from the injury inflicted on the African race in the slave-holding states.

"If slavery," says the late Theodore Sedgwick, "be a bad thing for one half of the country, it must be for the whole, though not equally. If one half of the blood of the body politic be corrupted, it is impossible that the other should remain pure. There can be no such thing as extensive political evil existing in one part of a nation, without spreading its influence, in a greater or less degree, over the other, any more than there can be a great sore on a particular limb, without affecting the health of the whole body."—*Pub. and Priv. Econ.: vol.* 1, *p.* 248.

Dr. Bacon, one of the editors of the Independent, has recently presented this subject in a still more forcible manner:

"The perpetuated existence of slavery, as it *is* perpetuated in the states south and south-west of Pennsylvania, is a violation of the duties which these states owe to the other states of the Union. We of the free states have a right to complain of those states, for thus violating the duties of good neighborhood. What is it that they are doing? They are keeping—with a passionate and inflexible will they insist on keeping—some three millions of people, on the soil of the Union, in a condition of extreme intellectual and moral degradation. Their laws, instead of encouraging the improvement and gradual elevation of the servile class—instead of doing anything to humanize them, and to raise them out of their deep moral degradation—are sternly set the other way. Their laws deny to the slaves the right of acquiring or possessing property—which is the first great stimulus to civilized industry; and the same laws annihilate among them (so far as laws can accomplish so hideous a result) the Divine institution of marriage, the institution essential above all others, to the development of human affections and of moral sensibilities. Their laws, instead of making provision for educating the children of the enslaved population, and for training them into civilization and a capacity for complete freedom, are contrived for the very purpose of keeping that barbarous population in the same condition of barbarism, through successive generations. Those states, I say, have no right thus to breed up, from age to age, within the boundaries of our Union, great hordes of barbarians, degraded into the condition of well-fed and well-housed cattle, maddened with the ever growing sense of oppression, chafing against their bonds, ever ready to burst into conflagration and slaughter—the opprobrium, the peril, the clog, the weakness, the disease of our common country. We of the free states have no jurisdiction or authority by which we can redress the wrong; but the wrong we suffer is no less a wrong because we cannot help ourselves. We have no right of intervention, but we have a right to feel the wrong and to express our sense of it."—*Ind.: June* 10, 1852.

Never was there a greater mistake than this, of supposing that the effects of slavery can be so completely confined to the South, as to relieve the North of all solicitude and responsibility on the subject. There are several reasons why the free states can never cease to remonstrate against slavery.

1. The first is the common right of benevolent regard. As freemen and as Christians we ought to desire the welfare of all men, and to promote that welfare to the utmost of our ability. Good will and philanthropy are not limited to state lines, nor are they excluded by disfranchising constitutions and laws. Human sympathy cannot be blighted in this way—it will act in favor of the oppressed, and overleap all the barriers which wicked legislation can interpose. Those who think to shut up our charities, and abridge our interest in the common brotherhood of man, have plainly miscalculated both their own ability and the character of those with whom they have to contend. Men may hold

slaves, but they can do no more; the power which would make them secure and give them public respect is not theirs, and never can be. All men will have a natural right to remonstrate against the crime, and the instinct of self-preservation will prompt them to do whatever they can for its extirpation.

2. Slavery impairs the moral sense of even the non-slave-holding states. It is a misfortune to become familiar with crime—it weakens the moral sense. Especially is this true where the crime is of a disputed character, and exists under cover of law. To witness continually the operation of such injustice—to see millions of unoffending men and women degraded to the condition of brutes, being bought and sold like cattle in the market, and all this under the sanction of law—cannot fail to mislead at least the unwary. Long acquaintance with the evil blunts those finer sensibilities on which virtuous action mainly depends, and leaves the individual, or the community, in a great measure callous to right impressions. Proximity to slavery is, therefore, dangerous to the free, and the depression of moral feeling which has thus been occasioned throughout the non-slave-holding states, is one of the saddest consequences that could possibly have happened to the North. Were money or mere physical suffering the only things involved by this "entangling alliance," it would be well, but moral deterioration is the inevitable result of such connec-

tions. Hence the North must either extinguish slavery, or be fatally corrupted by it. As a matter of sheer self-protection, the discusion must be kept up, and every means employed for the extinction of slavery that philanthropy and religion can devise.

3. Slavery endangers our national peace. Of all the exciting causes which have ever threatened the existence of this nation, slavery is the most fearful. Indeed, there is scarcely any other subject of difference, which can be said to have a national character. Other matters are mostly of a local nature, and admit of easy adjustment, but this scatters its poisonous influence through all the ramifications of government, and if not arrested, will ultimately destroy the noblest political system the world has ever known. On this account, if no other, the free states are deeply concerned in everything pertaining to slavery. When the Union was formed, by the adoption of the present constitution, most of the states—all but Massachusetts—were slave-holding states; it was, in fact, a union of slave-holding states, and the evils which now press upon us did not exist. But the lapse of more than sixty years has changed the aspect of affairs, and compromises which were tolerable then are intolerable now. States, which for fifty years have been free—states, several of which individually contain almost as large a population as the whole Union at the time of its formation—cannot readily acquiesce in arrangements made under circumstances so widely

different, and so totally inapplicable to their present condition. Slavery, while it was a common misfortune, could be borne with a better grace; but since the more prosperous members of the republic have thrown it off, and demonstrated that it may safely be dispensed with, to insist upon its continuance, and to exact for it all the concessions which it gained in an earlier day, is to provoke an opposition that must end either in the subversion of slavery or of the general government. Freemen will not bow their necks to the yoke; they choose to exert their influence for the removal of the evil, rather than bear the burden which it imposes.

4. The North, by keeping silent on this subject, would not only be involved in the guilt of conniving at oppression, but also in the guilt of betraying a most sacred trust—its knowledge of the superior advantages of freedom. The southern states have never known what it is to be free; to them, emancipation appears in the light of a dangerous experiment. Northern silence would be a tacit confirmation of these fears; it would say that we have no confidence in our own system, and no wish to extend it to them. It would be an unbrotherly act on the part of the free states, to allow the slave states to grope on forever in the darkness and guilt of slavery, without even attempting to relieve them. The South may make no demand for this fraternal assistance—nay, it may positively remonstrate against it, but this alters not the case. Christian

philanthropy waits not for a call, it is self-moved towards every scene of distress, and persists in its kind offices, though often repulsed. How else would Christian missions have been established among heathen nations? Not unfrequently have these missionaries fallen victims to the ferocity of those whom they sought to reform, but the martyrdom of some has not deterred others from the enterprise, nor has it ever been deemed a sufficient reason for abandoning the heathen world to its fate. In like manner, slave-holders may repel the philanthropic efforts of Northern freemen and Christians, yet, if animated by the spirit of their Master, they shall not fail nor be discouraged, till they have "set judgment in the earth."

5. Again, the free states are pervaded by the spirit of liberty so fully, that they can never brook the institution of slavery. For, although the paralyzing influence of the system may be felt disastrously among us, yet its utter injustice and stark contrariety to the most cherished sentiments of freemen, will always produce abhorrence in the better class of minds. Besides, it is the business of freemen to promote freedom. This they do not so much by openly attacking slavery, as by silently building up their own free and freedom-giving institutions, and establishing, practically, the right of every man to be a man. States which feel compelled thus to foster liberty, must always be sapping the foundations of tyranny. They can only be true

to themselves, so long as their acts tend to the subversion of political inequality and injustice. Necessity is, therefore, laid upon the free states to make war upon slavery; they must do it both in self-defence and in obedience to the dictates of truth and righteousness.

6. Another cause of agitation, and the most sovereign of all, is the stern demand of moral principle. Honest men cannot approve of robbing. The North cannot wink at the cruel injustice perpetrated upon the negro. Much less, can Northern men put forth their hands to aid in the abominable work. They must and will bear their testimony against the abuse, regardless of the consequences.

In view of these facts, we can see no prospect of a speedy settlement, or indeed, of any settlement of this question, short of the extinction of slavery. Christianity, in the providence of God, has aroused the consciences of men, and they cannot be quieted by the customary opiate — expediency. The virtue of this drug seems to be exhausted, and the somnolency which it once produced, does not return. Under this awakened state of public sentiment, compromises are no longer a finality. This is plainly not the day for compromises on moral questions. People are enquiring not only for what *is*, but also, and more ardently, for what *is right*. It is felt to be not enough that the African be left where he is — crushed and forlorn, scattered and peeled by centuries of oppression. There is manifestly springing up a tenderness towards the race, as one long misused, and it is possible that they may yet be fully brought within the pale of human sympathy. Kindly feelings, at all events, are prevailing in the hearts of many Northern men; they cannot see three millions of beings converted into brutes, without protesting against the infamous abuse. In short, slavery, blessed and baptized though it may be by those who practice it, is generally viewed by the people of the free states, as unmitigated villany. The negro whose ignorance and imbecility should entitle him to compassion, and especially exempt him from becoming the prey of honorable men, is summarily trodden down and cut off from all the rights of manhood; but this thing is not now done in a corner, nor with the consent of all who witness it; when the iron enters the colored man's soul he suffers not alone—intelligent Christian men share with him the pang, and appeal to Heaven in his behalf. A feeling of brotherhood is stirred, and it has fairly arrested the slave-holder in his career; it demands not only a reason for the cruelties inflicted, but also a reparation of injuries. It demands that the slave, being a man, shall be treated as a man.

CHAPTER XVI.

POSSIBLE RESULTS.

PERHAPS it is the design of Providence, that American slavery shall be the occasion of developing a principle new to the political world, though not new to Christianity, namely, the equality of races as well as of nations. The equality of nations or governments has long been admitted, but particular races have preyed upon each other. That there is an essential brotherhood of man—that the whole human race constitutes but one family—that every man is the brother of every other man—are great truths, well understood in religion, but strangely at variance with the political history of the world. In our own national history, the right of individuals of the same race—of white men—to strike for their liberty, is fully recognized, in opposition to the despotisms of the old world; yet we have not conceded the same right to other races. The African who aims at freedom we deem guilty of a high misdemeanor! We justly encourage European peasants to resist oppression, and then most shamefully turn to the negro in our midst and degrade him to the condition of a chattel. Such inconsistency has neither parallel nor excuse.

It may be, also, that the scarcely disguised infidelity—the bold denial of the higher law, as connected with civil government—is but a timely recall of the church and the country to the ancient landmarks, preparatory to new trials and new triumphs. Certainly no ground can be ceded here. The higher law is first, midst, and last. It is the sum total of all authority, because on it rests whatever of obligation can be found in any human law. So vital is this doctrine of the Divine supremacy, that with it must stand or fall not only civil liberty, but religion itself. It is true beyond all contradiction, 1. That no man can preach the gospel without preaching the higher law; 2. That no man can believe in God without believing in the higher law; 3. That no man can be a Christian without keeping the higher law. The burden of every Christian prayer is that the higher law may be established; that the kingdom of God may come, and his will be done on earth as it is in heaven. This loyalty to God is the substance of religion. It cannot be eradicated from the believer's heart without destroying the very substance of his faith, and cutting off all his hopes. It may be, we say, that this violent assault upon the first principles of religion is intended to awaken the church, more than ever, to its Divine allegiance, and its distinctive character as a purely theocratic institution.

But more than this. May we not hope that the thorough christianization of civil government is to be the issue of this great struggle? The permanence of our republic depends upon the realization of this hope. The crimes of our country, especially towards the African, if persevered in, will plunge it into ruin; it cannot escape the common fate of evil-doers. While penning these lines, there comes to me a speech of Kossuth, so full and so just on this point, that I beg the reader's indulgence for an extract:

"There is one law, the obedience to which would prove a rock upon which the freedom and happiness of nations may rest sure to the end of their days. And that law, ladies and gentlemen, is the law proclaimed by our Saviour; that rock is the unperverted religion of Christ. But while the consolation of this sublime truth falls meekly upon my soul, like as the moonlight falls upon the smooth sea, I humbly claim your forbearance, ladies and gentlemen; I claim it in the name of the Almighty Lord, to hear from my lips a mournful truth. It may displease you; it may offend; but still, truth is truth. Offended vanity may blame me; power may frown at me, and pride may call my boldness arrogant, but still, truth is truth, and I, bold in my unpretending humility, will proclaim that truth; I will proclaim it from land to land, and from sea to sea; I will proclaim it with the faith of the martyrs of old, till the seed of my word falls upon the consciences of men. Let come what come may: I say, with Luther, God may help me, I cannot otherwise. Yes, ladies and gentlemen, the law of our Saviour, the religion of Christ, can secure a happy future to nations. But, alas! there is yet no Christian people on earth — not a single one amongst all. I have spoken the word. It is harsh, but true. Nearly two thousand years have passed since Christ proclaimed the eternal decree of God, to which the happiness of mankind is bound, and sanctified it with his own blood, and still there is not one single nation on earth which would have enacted into its law-book that eternal decree. Men believe in the mysteries of religion according to the creed of their church; they go to church, and they pray, and give alms to the poor, and drop the balm of consolation into the wounds of the afflicted, and believe to do all what the Lord commanded to do, and believe to be Christians. No! Some few may be, but their nation is not—their country is not. The era of Christianity has yet to come, and when it comes, then, only then, will be the future of nations sure. Far be it from me to misapprehend the immense benefit which the Christian religion, such as it already is, has operated in mankind's history. It has influenced the private character of man, and the social condition of millions; it was the nurse of a new civilization, and softening the manners and morals of men, its influence has been felt even in the worst quarter of history—in war. The continual massacres of the Greek and Roman kings and chiefs, and the extermination of nations by them—the all-devastating warfare of the Timurs and Gengiskhans—are in general not more to be met with. But though that beneficial influence of Christianity we have cheerfully to acknowledge, yet it is still not to be disputed that the law of Christ does yet nowhere rule the Christian world."—*Speech at the Tabernacle, N. Y., June 21.*

To cover up sin is not the way to prosperity. With whatever facility we may barter the rights of the negro by way of compromise, the stability of the government gains nothing. Such policy only deceives. It removes not the evil, and its apparent success is no more an evidence of national security than the hectic flush upon the consumptive's countenance is a proof of health. Our safety, and our only safety, is in bringing, as speedily as possible, the principles of the government into exact conformity to the gospel. When this is done, heaven will be for us and not against us—its providence will cease to trouble us, and will surely discomfit our foes.

The danger occasioned by the anti-Christian treatment which our government inflicts on the negro, was never more clearly expressed than by Mr. Jefferson:

"Can the liberties of a nation be thought secure, when we have removed their only firm basis—a conviction in the minds of the people that these liberties are of the gift of God? That they are not to be violated but with his wrath? Indeed, I tremble for my country when I reflect that God is just; that his justice cannot sleep forever; that, considering numbers, nature, and natural means only, a revolution of the wheel of fortune, an exchange of situation is among possible events; that it may become probable by supernatural interference! The Almighty has no attribute which can take side with us in such a contest.

"What an incomprehensible machine is man! who can endure imprisonment, and death itself, in vindication of his own liberty, and the next moment be deaf to all those motives, whose power supported him through his trial, and inflict on his fellow men a bondage, one hour of which is fraught with more misery than that which he rose in rebellion to oppose. But we must wait with patience the workings of an overruling Providence, and hope that that is preparing the deliverance of these, our suffering brethren. When the measure of their tears shall be full—when their tears shall have involved heaven itself in darkness—doubtless a God of justice will awake to their distress, and by diffusing a light and liberality among their oppressors, or at length, by his exterminating thunder, manifest his attention to things of this world, and that they are not left to the guidance of blind fatality."—*Letter to M. Warville, Paris,* 1788.

But if the evangelization of civil government be too much to be expected at present, we may at least, confidently anticipate that this conflict will result in the emancipation of the colored race. The discussion—barren as it seems to many, of beneficial effects—has already done much towards accomplishing this object. True, there has been a temporary tightening of slave bonds in consequence of agitation; the oppressor, now, as of old, disregarding the command to let the people go, has actually increased their hardships. This, however, no more proves that the final issue of the movement will not be favorable, than any disagreeable sensation produced by medicine proves that its ultimate effect will not be salutary. Some incidental evils always accompany the work of improvement. He who is disheartened at such trials, does not understand the economy of reform. If we wait till slave-holders concur, we shall wait forever. Such prudence would leave every perpetrator of crime undisturbed, because the guilty never like to be exposed. The work is to be done in spite of opposition; not by deferring it till all opposition has ceased. Among the most favorable indications, is the fact that the subject of slavery has at last fairly got into Congress. The operation of gag laws could not keep it out. Neither the extreme dread of the South to touch the subject, nor the persevering neglect of the North to give consequence to anti-slavery movements, could check the progress of sentiment, or prevent its approach to the capitol. The spell is broken. Congress cannot avoid the subject if it would. In more than half the states an anti-slavery feeling has become ubiquitous, and no possible circumstances can confine this feeling to northern latitudes. It will flow out in all directions; it will pervade the slave states as it does the free, and the halls of legislation as it does the social circle. Happy would it be, if the representatives of the people were better prepared for this contingency.

Extraordinary pains have been taken to put down all agitation. We have heard again and again of the great delicacy of the subject. Slavery must not be discussed, because slave-holders would not endure it. That time has passed, and the government still survives; and that it will still survive the most thorough discussion, as well as the most radical improvement in this matter, we have not the slightest doubt. Why should it not? There is certainly no one aspect of the question either impracticable, or fraught with injury to the South. Emancipation, notwithstanding the difficulties which some have seen in the way, is one of the most practicable suggestions ever made for a nation's welfare. Let us look at a few facts.

1. If the slaves were white men, there would not be a single objection to their emancipation. All would admit that our three millions of slaves ought to be freed at once, and that they could just as well take care of themselves as can any other three millions of white men.

2. The slaves, when emancipated, will be more easily governed than they are now, for the simple reason, that they will be in their natural place in society; they will act as human beings, and be acted upon by the law as human beings; they will have character, and responsibilities, and immunities, which will elicit in them, as in other men, due regard to conduct. In a word, they will have the motives to govern them that other people have.

3. The slaves, when freed, will be even more useful to the white population among whom they live. It is notorious that slave labor is the dearest labor which can be employed. The extreme poverty of the southern states is mainly owing to this. The men who till the soil have no sufficient interest in their work, and hence the country must always be depressed. Could these colored people be edu-

cated and hired, as laborers are in the free states, their skill and efficiency would soon enrich their employers.

4. Emancipation will be no less safe than profitable. The idea of danger is utterly absurd—the negroes would be as harmless as they now are, and more so. In the West Indies, where emancipation has been tried, it has led to no disorder—the poor colored man has proved as quiet as the poor white man. The South would be abundantly more secure in every respect, if all her slaves were raised from the irresponsibility of brutes to the responsibility of men. It avails nothing to say that slaves are ignorant—can neither read nor write—for this is precisely the condition of thousands of white people in this and every other country. Many of our best farmers and mechanics have no education. The slaves know enough to work, and it would be well if many of their owners knew as much.

5. Oppression and degradation are provocatives to sedition and insurrection. Let the galling chains of the slave be broken off, and let his attachments be those of kind and honorable dealing, and we hazard nothing in saying that he will be orderly and confiding. This is the way to remove the perils of a slave-holding community. That the South is in danger, may be true, but if so, it is a danger created by its wickedness, and the only means of giving security is to banish the tyranny from which the danger arises.

6. From the abolition of slavery, the South has everything to hope and nothing to fear. Not only would the state of society be rendered more secure, but its property would be vastly augmented. The rise of land alone, would, in a single year, more than counterbalance all the nominal losses—for real losses there can be none—occasioned by emancipation. Lands now worth from three to ten dollars per acre, would then be worth from fifty to one hundred dollars per acre. Besides, the slaves would be worth infinitely more to the country. Not a dollar of property would be sacrificed by ceasing to reckon men as money. Those who have lands should be made to set their slaves free, and find the remuneration in the incrased value of their real estate, while those who own nothing but negroes should be indemnified to some extent by the state, through a tax levied on those who hold other kinds of property. If cupidity were a ruling motive with slave-holders, they would be gainers by promoting emancipation.

7. So impressed are we with the force of these truths, that we believe the South not only ought to tolerate discussion on the subject of slavery, but should actually hire men to proclaim anti-slavery doctrines through all her territory. Instead of persecuting abolitionists, the slave states should pay them a liberal salary, and increase their number as fast as possible. Emancipation is a blessing for which those states might pay millions, and yet be

gainers; it would be to them political salvation. But great as the advantage would be, we may not force it upon them—we are limited to that expostulation and fraternal entreaty which man owes to man. From the faithful discharge of this duty, there can be no release.

CHAPTER XVII.

CONCLUSION.

I HAVE now only to suggest certain causes, which, whatever may be the present aspects or future results of this great controversy, must inevitably keep it before the people for yet a considerable time. No "finality" has been reached, or can be reached, till the demand created by these causes is complied with. Men may as well legislate against the tides of "old ocean," as against the essential elements of their own humanity. Nature knows no compromises. Nor are these causes confined to the free states. They belong to man as man; to the freeman, the slave, and the slave-holder; to all ages, and all countries.

1. The abolition of slavery is demanded by eternal justice. This is our answer to all who ask a reason for emancipation. What justice demands, it can never be safe or expedient to withhold. If God had not made the negro a man, his down-trodden condition would have made no appeal to heaven—none to earth. It would not have proclaimed injury, fraud, usurpation, and cruelty, perpetrated

by man upon his fellow man, without the slightest wish or intention ever to make restitution. Slavery is thus in conflict with the very foundation principle of all order. It strikes down both the government of God and the government of man. By making a mockery of justice, it arrays itself against the slave-holder no less than against the slave. It vainly attempts to change the type of nature, and blot out elements which the Creator has made perpetual. Hence, so long as man is man, this war of right against wrong must of necessity continue—he is constitutionally pledged to "fight a good fight" in this holy cause. To be indifferent here, is to sink below the dignity of nature, and take a position, which, though lawful to brutes, is not to man.

2. Every other attribute of God demands the abolition of slavery. His wisdom, benevolence, holiness and power, are equally opposed to the degradation inflicted upon the negro, who, no less than the white man, was made in his image, and is the work of his hands. Slavery may work, but God is counter-working; his wisdom and power, his holiness and eternity, are a guarantee that the machinations of the wicked shall not succeed. It matters not how men compromise. They may say, "We have made a covenant with death, and with hell are we at agreement; when the overflowing scourge shall pass through, it shall not come unto us, for we have made lies our refuge, and under falsehood have we hid ourselves." But God says, "Judgment will I

lay to the line, and righteousness to the plummet; and the hail shall sweep away the refuge of lies, and the waters shall overflow the hiding place: your covenant with death shall be disannulled, and your agreement with hell shall not stand." Statesmen may toil assiduously, and lay their plans with profound skill, and the people may bring their most costly offerings to the shrine of union, but all to no purpose: for over every nation that will not do right, "the line of confusion and the stones of emptiness" are stretched by an invisible, but Almighty hand, and there is no escape. Anti-slavery lecturers are only an echo of Providence, and if they should cease to speak, the truths which they announce will still be uttered, but the disasters attendant on vice will speak in far less kindly tone. If such lecturers trouble Israel, it is only as the faithful utterances of Elijah troubled Ahab.

3. The abolition of slavery is demanded by the spirit of the age. It is extremely absurd to continue at this day and in this country, an institution befitting only the midnight of pagan darkness. When nations were wholly barbarous—when neither science nor religion had shed its mitigating influence on society, such flagrant injustice might be tolerated, but to attempt it now is infatuation. Something may be achieved, it is true, by spreading a thick pall of darkness over large sections of country—that is, by keeping society still in barbarism; yet even this device is about to fail. The age

is happily too full of light to admit of easy circumscription. The spirit of progress stamps slavery as an impossibility. We must either return to savage life, or dismiss this relic of uncultivated and un-Christianized times.

4. The abolition of slavery is demanded by the character of our own government. It is in vain to rely on compromises and exceptions, when the whole spirit and substance of our republican system is directly hostile to slavery. The more we sustain freedom for ourselves, the more we sustain it for others; republicanism, therefore, disqualifies its possessors for enacting or executing oppressive laws. Never was slavery more out of its place than in this country. It is an exotic on our free shores, and must die because it cannot live in an atmosphere of liberty.

5. The abolition of slavery is demanded by common sense. Slavery is not simply wicked—it does not accomplish its ends by merely unjustifiable means. It evinces everywhere extreme imbecility. In whatever light we view it, it is a thoroughly contemptible arrangement. So long as man is rational, he must, apart from all moral considerations, despise a system which, under the pretence of doing good, inflicts only evil. God has given men too much sense, to admit of such stupidity. Slavery sinks below the intellectual, as it does below the moral powers of man; it belongs to the category of crime—a department in which folly

and guilt are always combined. If we cannot have something better than slavery, by way of civil regulation, let us have nothing. The human mind spurns such nonsense. Reason demands reasonable laws, or none; it insists on equity, or an abandonment of the functions of legislation.

www.ingramcontent.com/pod-product-compliance
Lightning Source LLC
LaVergne TN
LVHW011216110826
845150LV00006B/1437

* 9 7 8 1 4 2 5 5 1 6 9 8 7 *